Lucia Vriends-Parent

Beagles

Everything about Purchase, Care, Nutrition,
Breeding, Behavior, and Training

With Color Photographs by well-known Photographers
and Drawings by Michele Earle-Bridges

Consulting Editor: Matthew M. Vriends, Ph.D.

BARRON'S

New York • London • Toronto • Sydney

Photo credits
Eugene Butenas (LCA Photography): page 63, page 35, top; back cover, top right.
Wim van Vugt: front cover; inside front cover; page 17; page 18; page 35, bottom; page 36; page 53; page 54; page 64; inside back cover; back cover, top left and bottom.

For my daughter Tanya, with love.

All inquiries should be addressed to:
Barron's Educational Series, Inc.
250 Wireless Boulevard
Hauppauge, NY 11788

International Standard Book No. 0-8120-3829-0

Library of Congress Catalog Card No. 87-26641

Library of Congress Cataloging-in-Publication Data

Vriends-Parent, Lucia.
  Beagles : everything about purchase, care, nutrition, breeding, behavior, and training.

  Includes index.
  1. Beagles (Dogs) I. Title.
SF429.B3V74   1987   636.7'53   87-26641
ISBN 0-8120-3829-0

PRINTED IN HONG KONG

123   490   98765

Advice and Warning:
This book is concerned with selecting, keeping, and raising beagles. The publisher and the author think it is important to point out that the advice and information for beagle maintenance applies to healthy, normally developed animals. Anyone who acquires an adult dog or one from an animal shelter must consider that the animal may have behavioral problems and may, for example, bite without any visible provocation. Such anxiety-biters are dangerous for the owner as well as the general public.

  Caution is further advised in the association of children with dogs, in meetings with other dogs, and in exercising the dog without a leash.

Contents

Preface

While I'm writing these introductory remarks, my eight-year-old beagle Storm is relaxing in a chair, *her* chair to be precise. Her mischievous pitch-dark eyes are gazing at me. I look at her. A first-class example of a contented dog—or so I think.

"What makes me and so many other fanciers so interested in beagles?" I ask myself. I reply by recounting their good traits: they are relatively calm and even-tempered and always ready to keep you company. Beagles have a "sweet hunting voice," as they say in the trade. They are seldom noisy; only when left alone against their will do they tend to howl loudly. They are kind to other pets—although they may sometimes forget themselves and start to think of a cat or hamster as prey. Then their hunting instincts take over and they chase the other animals like crazy! The result may be a broken plate or vase that got in the way. They also are affectionate toward children. And, generally, they are extremely intelligent and merry.

Still, beagles aren't animals that will accept everything from everyone. They can be stubborn—but actually I like that in a dog. It shows character.

I could continue in this vein. If I did, the sum of the traits I would list still wouldn't really explain why beagles are so popular. There are many other dog breeds with similar good traits. I know that a completely satisfying answer is impossible to give. It's just as hard as trying to define what it is like to be in love.

This book is based on many years of experience with beagles and on a careful study of beagle biology and genetics. In the pages that follow you will share the experiences of beagle fanciers around the world, as many of the facts in this book are based on an interesting correspondence I have maintained with experts in England, Sweden, South Africa, the Netherlands, and the United States. I am grateful for the help.

I will try to answer many common questions, but I can't cover every possible question. Who could? As you become more experienced, you will draw your own conclusions from observations and comparisons. If you have had success with a tried-and-true method, don't switch just because I'm suggesting something different. That would be unwise! You will continue to learn through loving and appreciative interaction with your dogs, even though you will find that many of your conclusions lead only to new questions.

Don't forget that, as a pet owner, it is *you* who takes on the responsibility of caretaker, not the other way around. We take the dogs into our homes, and we must provide the care. At the core of the relationship is the love of the owners for their dogs. This love is the basis of the joy you derive from your dogs. Love implies care, and whatever care you lavish on your dogs will be returned by them many times over.

I am particularly grateful to my husband, the biologist Dr. Matthew M. Vriends, who brings more than 35 years of experience to the field. I am also thankful to my friend, fellow biologist, and compatriot, Mr. Max B. Heppner, M.Sc., of Baltimore, Maryland, for his invaluable assistance in the preparation of the text; and to John Mandeville, Director of Judging Research and Development, American Kennel Club.

All the opinions and conclusions expressed in the following pages are my own, however, and any errors must be my own responsibility.

Lucia Vriends-Parent
Loveland, Ohio
September, 1987

Considerations Before You Buy

Is a Beagle Right For You?

So you have decided to buy a beagle! Or is it just an impulse, not a real decision? It is extremely important to know the difference.

There are many good reasons to acquire a beagle, but there are even more good reasons not to get one. A beagle is not an easy pet to keep. It requires a lot from you. You have to remain devoted for 12 to 15 years or more and provide constant good, and therefore expensive care. Count on spending at least an hour a day of your personal attention and at least a dollar a day of your hard-earned cash.

If other people will be involved, you have to be sure that they are emotionally and reasonably prepared to take on a beagle and understand what will be required of them. The person who will bear the primary responsibility for the chores of maintaining the dog should get first consideration. All too often these chores may stick like a bone in his or her throat.

There are hundreds of cases in which someone gets carried away with an emotional burst of love for a puppy. He or she boasts to the people in the office about the newly acquired beagle—how exceptionally affectionate it is, or what a splendid country dog, or what an adaptable city dog that knows how to handle life in an apartment ten floors up in the heart of town.

Or maybe it's a girl of nine who pesters the rest of the family about wanting a small, cuddly puppy, one of those cute little beagles from the litter produced by the dog owned by her best friend. Dad and Mom give in to her declared love of pets, and a beagle comes into the household.

You need to be clearheaded about your decision, because acquiring a beagle isn't like buying a computer. You can't just turn it on when you need it. Dad and Mom may like the idea of owning a dog. Daughter may even like to cuddle it when the mood strikes her. But someone must accept the cold reality of pet ownership. Someone must be there when it comes to wiping up a puddle, brushing a coat, going for an airing, fighting an attack of fleas, running to the vet, and similar unavoidable requirements of pet ownership. Especially the walking, the walking, and more walking!

To the person who accepts overall responsibility, a beagle is like a baby in the house who isn't toilet trained. A puppy requires almost the same amount of care as a demanding, whining, yelping, slobbery, and wet little child. (Some even say a baby is easier than a puppy.) It isn't the puppy's fault, of course. It didn't ask to be taken into the house.

You get the point! Never mind that some member of the household decides that he or she can't live without a beagle. The one who should have the deciding vote is the individual who will care for the dog. If it is he or she who wants the beagle, it will be all right.

If the decision to buy isn't properly made, the dog is the biggest loser. Generally what happens is that the poor puppy is sent from one family that is not prepared to care for it to another equally unprepared. It winds up neurotic and unmanageable.

Key Questions About Obtaining a Beagle

When you get the idea you might want a beagle, first and foremost take the time for calm reflection. Get all the information you can. Read books about dog care, go to dog shows, and talk to beagle owners.

The next step is to think again. Think about your acquisition as a hypersensitive, emotionally vulnerable, dependent living being that looks up to you as the Big Boss. A beagle is not a car that you can trade in after four years or so. It is a living responsibility that stays with you longer than 12 years on the average.

So again the key question is, *why* do you want that beagle?

The next question, just as important, is what do you do with it after you get it? What's your lifestyle? What are your finances? How much room can you give it? How much time do you have, and how much do you want to spend on the dog? How much persistence do you have? What's the reaction of other people in the house? Also, what's the reaction of other *animals* in the house? Do you have a cat, a budgie, or a hamster? Remember, the dog you're considering is a breed that was originally developed for trailing rabbits and hares and can make your sweet cat or hamster as nervous as well, a cat.

Another point to consider may surprise you: perhaps you ought to get *two* beagles! Remember, beagles are pack dogs. If you think that your work or other duties may keep you from spending enough time with your dog, two dogs may help solve your problem! Truly, two beagles don't make much more work than one. Here again, the deciding factor may be whether you have enough space, money, and the like.

If you decide in favor of just one puppy, remember that it will consider you one of its own kind. Like other hunting hounds, the beagle is intelligent. You will have to deal with it sternly from the first day on, so that the young animal knows who is boss.

More Thoughts About Space

Don't just consider yourself, consider your dog when you think about space. You want your dog to be happy. If you have a one-bedroom apartment on the tenth floor, you don't buy a Great Dane, Doberman pinscher, or German shepherd. I'm not just referring to physical space alone. Quality space is important too.

Let me speak from personal experience and tell you that the dogs I've kept always had the most fun, expressed themselves most fully, and stayed the healthiest if I could give them proper room. My line of work caused me to live in many different countries in a variety of situations. I have lived in an apartment in The Hague (the Netherlands), in a marvelous old Victorian home in Florida with plenty of grounds around it, in a condo in Adelaide (Australia), and in a suburban home near Cincinnati, Ohio. Whenever I moved, my dogs went along.

With all that experience, the first thing I did when I moved to Loveland was to fence in a large part of the yard. I had the room, and I wanted to give the dogs a chance to run free. With all the traffic, there really was little choice, because a beagle never denies its origins. A healthy, active beagle remains a hunting hound forever.

In sum, the ideal situation is to give your beagle a fenced-in yard. Still, if you live in an apartment, you can find ways to indulge your desire to keep a beagle. Basically, this means that you have to count on walking your dog at least an hour per day. On your days off, you will have to take it along to a park or the beach, where it can run off its almost boundless energy.

If you have the time and are willing to devote it to your beagle, you'll be well rewarded by this extremely friendly breed that seems ever ready to play. I have found the breed to love family life. I look forward to winter evenings when I have the fireplace burning. My dogs come to lie beside me cosily, and we can spend hours staring into the flames. They don't move a muscle while they rest their beagle faces on my lap. Maybe they dream of hunting grounds that swarm with rabbits and raccoons!

Male or Female?

How do we pick a puppy? Should it be female or a male? If you have any thought of raising a litter some day, then the choice is already determined for you: You'll have to get a female. Of course, the breeding business involves males as well, but the owner of a male dog can only observe from a distance how the mother cares for the puppies.

If breeding isn't among your plans, you can consider either sex. Males generally grow up to be larger and tougher. My experience indicates that at some point, a male dog will test his power with you and see if he can boss you. A female seldom does this, although a female beagle is more likely to try it than a female dog of another breed.

Considerations Before You Buy

The independent spirit of beagle males can be real trouble, especially if a female in heat (*estrus*) is in the neighborhood. The odor pulls him irresistibly to the home of the female, where he may spend hours, even days. Generally, this goes along with a miserable-sounding mating call. This attracts other males, who join in the howling, which is hardly a pleasure for the owner of the female. Meanwhile, you have to do without the company of your beagle.

The situation doesn't have to degenerate to this point, however. If you have trained your dog to respond to your call, you can call him back and suppress his wanderlust. Better yet, don't let your dog out of the house unless you have him on a leash.

It is easier to keep a female at home. Females have a yen to roam only when they are in heat, and most of them are in heat only twice a year, on the average. At that time, there will be some bloody discharge from her vagina for 7–10 days. You may want to get the right kind of sanitary napkin from the veterinarian, or you can make do by washing the bedding in the sleeping basket more frequently. If the discharge soils the carpet and furniture, you will have to get sanitary napkins.

In short, males are generally more independent and can be headstrong now and then. First, males are more watchful. Don't be surprised, however, if your male beagle quickly warms up to a stranger. He may bark a few times, but then he will start wagging his tail and seem to say, "I don't know you, but I sure would like to be your friend!"

By the way, with your veterinarian's consent, you can give chlorophyll tablets to your female dog when she is in estrus, which will help to neutralize the scent of the female secretions that attract male dogs. A veterinarian will also be able to give your female dog hormone injections. However, some practitioners now discourage this practice, and the consensus is that it should be avoided if at all possible because of the possibility of long-term negative side effects (hormonal imbalances and related health problems).

The Dog Trade

You can't pick up a beagle just anywhere. You need to take some care. The best source is a reputable pet store or a reputable breeder. Many pet stores are extremely responsible and have good-looking puppies that are well cared for. Others, unfortunately, market the produce of so-called "puppy mills." These operations, which breed without planning, usually mate any available female with any available male. As long as both parents are beagles, they think, the pups will be beagles, too. They don't discriminate and proceed without attention to proper appearance, character, and genetic defects. Volume is the only motivation. Beagle females go into estrus twice a year, and therefore they are bred twice a year. If production in the puppy mill lags, the female is sold.

After you have determined the source of your puppy, be sure that you acquire the right paperwork, including pedigree and vaccinations. Buy with care and forethought. Don't buy on impulse, or you may get into the same difficulty as a man who called me one day for advice.

"I'm calling you on the advice of the president of our local beagle club. He said you have a litter of puppies for sale. What's the best way to get to your house?"

I gave him the directions, but mentioned that it would take at least another three weeks before the puppies could be taken from their mother. I also told him that I had already promised two of the puppies to another person.

"Well, to tell you the truth, I don't think I really want to drive 40 miles to get a puppy. I would go a few miles down the road, but not 40. Besides, I need to get a puppy by tomorrow. It's my son's birthday. He'll be eight years old."

I kept the conversation short by saying I was sorry, but I couldn't help him.

Several weeks later, I heard that the man who had called me proceeded to look through some newspaper ads until he found someone who would sell him a beagle puppy. He just had to have one

Considerations Before You Buy

for his young son. The puppy he came up with clearly was the product of a puppy mill. It was not in good health and totally lacked breed quality. It soon had to be taken to the veterinarian, and the bills were many times the purchase price of the puppy. After a few weeks, the man tried to take the dog back to the dealer, but he got nowhere. The sale was final, he was told.

The end of the story is that a poor, sick animal had to be taken to the pound. The eight-year-old boy received a computer as compensation. After all, he had to have something to play with!

Selecting a Breeder

If you decide to buy from a breeder, consult the experienced hands in your local beagle club and the representatives of the American Kennel Club. When you have found someone who seems good, take the trouble to confirm your selection.

Breeders who want only to sell puppies and show no interest in what you want to do with the puppy after you buy it are not the kind you should deal with. Expect the breeder to ask about the makeup of your family, your housing, and your plans. You may find that the breeder seems reluctant to sell if you live in a small apartment where it is hard to take walks every day. Others may prefer not to sell if you have a baby or toddlers at home.

Good breeders also take an interest in the quality of the puppy they sell you. They may ask you to take the animal to at least one dog show, so that the breeder's success can be measured by the decision of an impartial judge.

Often, a discussion between buyer and seller leads to a genuinely friendly understanding. That's fine, provided that you don't lose sight of the business aspects of the relationship. You have the right to see the various papers, and the breeder has the obligation to show them to you. Some breeders do this with pleasure and undisguised pride. Others refuse, or look for an excuse. If that happens, get back into your car and take your business elsewhere.

A purebred beagle comes with a registration certificate from the American Kennel Club, or at least an application form. This form must be filled in properly and forwarded to the AKC (see page 76). There should also be a pedigree and a health certificate signed by the veterinarian who has been taking care of the breeder's animals, including vaccinations. The registration certificate is an official AKC document. If the breeder has already named the puppy you picked and has registered it, you must register the transfer and send the certificate with the appropriate fee to the AKC. The AKC then transfers the puppy to your ownership and keeps a record of it. You receive a new certificate. If the breeder gives you only an application for registration, you should complete it as quickly as possible, giving the name you selected for the puppy. Mail the completed application with the appropriate fee to the AKC headquarters in New York.

Understand that the pedigree is only a chart giving the puppy's ancestry. It is not a part of its official papers. The health certificate, however, is official. It indicates precisely which shots have been given and on which dates the next shots are due. Your own veterinarian consults this health certificate the first time you bring in your new puppy, so that he or she can continue with the proper treatment begun under the care of the breeder. The health certificate also indicates on which day the animal was wormed.

You would do well to plan to view your prospective puppy's litter several times. You may be excited about your future pet, but don't make a definite selection before the puppies are eight to nine weeks old. Breeders generally do not require you to select from a litter that is much younger.

Usually, business is done on a first come, first served basis. You put your name on a waiting list, and your turn comes after the people whose names are higher on the list have had their turn. If your name tops the list, you have the choice of the litter. If you are, let's say, fourth on the list, then you can choose from all but the three puppies that have been sold or promised to another.

When the time comes, be sure you understand that you have the right to refuse to buy. The refusal can be based on a variety of circumstances. Perhaps the puppy doesn't appeal to you, or perhaps you've had another look around the kennel and things don't look right to you.

Your first visit should occur when the puppies are five to six weeks old. Your discussion with the breeder will tell you a lot. You should also pay attention to the female that mothered the litter and to other dogs on the premises. How do they act? Do they look well fed and well cared for? If they look good, the puppies are likely to be good. If the level of care is poor, then don't expect that the puppies will fare any better.

The condition of the kennel itself can tell you a lot about the care and attention the breeder gives to the dogs. Don't expect a superluxurious layout and a pressurized cleaning system. Not every breeder can afford this. But if, for example, the place is piled high with manure, look elsewhere for your puppy.

The puppies themselves should be the picture of health. By the time you make your choice, the eight-or nine-week-old puppies should be active and moving fairly fast. Sluggishness is a poor sign, unless the puppies have just finished a meal.

Selecting a Puppy

Good puppies should have meat on their frames, but their ribs should still be evident to the touch. Sunken flanks and spare ribs point to poor feeding. Round bellies, which usually mean swollen bellies, mostly point to an infestation of intestinal worms; nowadays this is unacceptable for puppies of that age.

Pay close attention to the body openings. There should be no feces stuck under the tails, a sign of diarrhea. In female puppies, the area around the vagina should be clean, as should the foreskin of males. The drooping, low-set ears should also look clean.

There should be no pronounced odor beyond the natural puppy smell. Pay especially close attention to the eyes. They must be clean, wet, shiny, smooth, and transparent. Too much moisture in the eyes is also undesirable. Tears running down the cheeks are a sign of a possible infection, or worse.

If you pick the most adventurous puppy of the litter, you run a greater chance that it will try to dominate you—meaning that you may well have obedience problems. Don't pick the smallest puppy. It was probably held back in its development because of poor health. Also, never choose a puppy that shyly hides in a corner. There is a chance that this puppy will develop into a frightened dog.

I would go for the puppy that is second or third to the most challenging and daring in the litter. Beagles are extremely inquisitive, even at an early age, and they very much like to be petted and fondled. That's another point to look for. Finally, check to see the puppy has a shiny coat and a nice color. I think that the tricolors are the most popular, but also attractive are the white with lemon or tan tigering, especially if they have a black nose and deep, dark eyes. Tan-and-white and lemon-and-white puppies are born almost completely white with a faint darker pattern like a jigsaw on the back and head. Tigering can be black marking on a blue ground, too. Other beagles are solid white, black or orange.

As soon as you have made your selection, it is a good idea to tattoo your beagle puppy on the inside of its ear. It is an even better idea to use an American Kennel Club registration number, since they will assist, when contacted (see address, page 76), in locating the dog's recorded owners. However, there is no requirement that a dog be tattooed to be registered or shown or to participate in any other AKC activity.

Taking the Puppy Home

The best procedure is to arrange the transfer of your new puppy in advance. That way, the breeder can take precautions that minimize the chance of car sickness. Food should be withheld from the puppy or it should be fed lightly four hours before you plan to pick it up. If you insist on selecting a puppy and taking it with you on the spot, the risk is yours.

Considerations Before You Buy

Everybody, including children, should learn how to hold a puppy. Place one hand against the rib cage, and support the puppy's rear end and paws with the other.

Take along some old blankets and towels. They will help protect the interior of the car from any possible vomit or saliva. If it will be a long trip, take a thermos with water and a watering bowl.

Start training your new puppy with the first ride in the car. Indicate the place where it is to sit now and in the future. In a stationwagon, put the puppy in the back. In a sedan, put the animal in the rear. Don't put it in the trunk, where you would lose all contact with the animal, and not be able to tell how it is behaving. Furthermore, it won't get enough fresh air.

Don't put your new puppy up front. Beagles are quite curious, which is appropriate for scent hounds (dogs that use their sense of smell while trailing game). They like to explore the car floor, which can be dangerous if they touch the brake or clutch during the trip. Furthermore, the dog should be kept away from the heat or air-conditioning vents. In the winter, the heated airflow can cause the dog to be overcome by heat. In the summer, the air-conditioning can cause stiff muscles.

Don't put the dog on the rear windowledge, either. This would pose life-threatening danger in case of a sudden stop that could cause the dog to fly through the interior against (perhaps even through) the windshield. There is also a good chance that the hurtling dog will strike the driver or passenger, causing further injuries.

Most dogs, including beagles, like to look out of the window during a car trip. That means they prefer sitting on a rear seat, rather than lying on the floor. For safety's sake, you can get a seat belt at the pet store that's designed specifically for dogs. Alternatively, you may use a carrier or crate. Should you decide to do so, make sure it is large enough for the puppy and that it provides adequate ventilation.

To train a new dog to ride on the back seat, take along a passenger for the first ride. That person can stroke the dog and talk to it encouragingly. At the same time, the passenger can keep the dog from gradually crawling closer and closer until it finally sits in a lap!

This may be unwise on the first ride, because the dog may then count on riding in someone's lap even when it is full-grown.

Some dogs keep having problems with carsickness. Your veterinarian has medicine for this condition, but it is healthier to get a dog gradually accustomed to riding in a car. Start during the first ride. Have your passenger keep a sharp eye on the puppy. If he or she notices any disquiet or salivation, stop the car immediately. Let the dog out for about 10 minutes, and then resume the journey.

You may have to stop several times during the first ride, but don't let that get you down. The trouble you take then will pay off later. As soon as your new puppy is used to its new home, you can gradually expose it to more car trips. Start with a short, one-minute ride, then increase it to two, five, and more minutes. This way, most puppies quickly get used to riding in cars and don't get carsick.

Once you get your new puppy home safely, let it reconnoiter in an area where there is no danger from passing automobiles. Give it plenty of time to urinate or defecate before you take it inside. At that point, the puppy becomes part of the family and it will be totally dependent on you for its education, feeding, care, management, and housing.

Basic Rules Of Beagle Care

Getting the Puppy Settled

You will probably have a basket ready for your new puppy, but before you introduce it there, let it become acquainted with the entire layout of your home. Everything is new to the puppy, and it will want to investigate everything with its nose and eyes. It has no time for anything else! Several hours may pass before it decides to look for a place to take a short rest. Soon it will be sniffling around again. Don't be surprised if the puppy's resting place is right in front of your feet. Especially during the first two days, the puppy will want to stay in your immediate vicinity.

The intensive sniffing can take several days, because, as I mentioned, the beagle puppy is a hunting hound. After four or five days, however, the puppy behaves as if it has lived with you for years. It knows all corners and openings and is especially familiar with places where it can look out of a window without losing its balance.

Those first few days, be sure to follow the feeding schedule and menu established by the breeder. If you want to change the diet, don't change it abruptly. Do it gradually over a period of several days to avoid diarrhea.

Housebreaking

All puppies need to be housetrained. This doesn't have to involve a big drama. Just count on spending a lot of time on the project for a week or two.

First, let the puppy out early each morning. Take it to the same spot, a section of lawn or whatever, where you will walk with it. You need to lead it, because it won't follow you on its own. This way, the puppy knows what you expect of it when you take it back to the same spot. In the beginning, you may have to take the puppy there every hour on the hour. At the very least, count on taking the puppy out after every meal and after every nap. There are also between-times when the puppy looks uneasy, sniffs, and walks in circles as if searching for something. Until three to six months of age, bladder control is not yet fully established. Therefore, you must learn to be alert to your dog's needs and the physical signs it gives you.

You will find that your beagle puppy wants to keep its own sleeping area clean. This desire is usually instilled in a dog by its mother while she is nursing the litter. Once she no longer takes responsibility for cleaning up after each puppy's eliminations, the mother generally makes it quite clear that she wants elimination removed from the "den". The puppies learn quickly to comply, or suffer swift correction. Your job is to pick up where the mother left off.

Elimination should be handled with common sense. Until a puppy truly understands what it is expected to do, accidents happen. These accidents are not evidence of willful misbehavior, so react swiftly, firmly, and fairly. To show your displeasure, "no" and an angry look should suffice. Then give the puppy a clear indication of the proper procedure.

Take the dog to the elimination area and praise it. Hitting the dog or rubbing its nose in the excrement are confusing and counterproductive. Clean each "accident" site to remove urine odor and avoid reattracting the dog to the spot. Use soapy water and a little vinegar or a special solution available at pet stores. Don't use household ammonia, which will only enhance the problem. (Ammonia in the urine attracts the dog to the spot in the first place.)

Don't overreact when you discover an unwanted deposit on your floor. Let the dog know you are displeased, but do this in a manner that the dog understands. Bring the dog to the spot, have it look at the excrement, point at it, and scold in a low, growling tone. Then put the dog in the proper elimination spot. When you return to the house, banish the dog to its sleeping area and clean up the mess out of the dog's sight. Eventually, even if it isn't caught in the act, the dog will comprehend your disapproval.

Basic Rules of Beagle Care

Crates

You need to take special precautions for the night. Dogs sleep enough during the day that they have energy left at night for taking a walk through the house. You can let older dogs do this without worry, but you need to guard against a puppy's making a puddle or pile somewhere in the house. You do this by shutting the puppy in a confined area — a small, uncarpeted room, a special cage, or a roomy crate. Suitable crates can be purchased in a pet shop. Don't make the mistake of thinking of the crate as a prison. Your beagle will probably accept it as a den — and a den is something to be kept clean. Don't place water or food bowls inside the crate.

Before you, yourself, turn in, take the dog for a last walk and then put it in the crate. Secure the door, and then you can go to sleep.

Maybe not for long! Puppies are used to having their mother and littermates around from the day they were born. They are used to the body heat put out by their family, which isn't available to them now. To keep the puppy warm in its box, put a hot water bottle inside it. If the bottle is quite warm, protect the puppy by wrapping an old blanket around the hot water bottle.

Whelping box and sleeping baskets. Make certain that the one you make or choose is large enough for a full-grown beagle to lie down in comfortably.

The puppy is also used to nocturnal sounds made by its dam and littermates. By contrast, your house may be quite silent once everyone has retired. You'll have to do something about that, too. A good method is to put a ticking clock outside the box. That accustoms the puppy to a monotonous, reassuring sound. Some dog fanciers say that the sound of the alarm clock is something like the beat of the mother dog's heart—a sound that the puppy has long been used to.

Place a few old blankets in the crate, so the puppy can bed down on something soft. With all that, you will have prepared the puppy for a good, restful night.

Still, many puppies seem to have trouble falling asleep the first few nights. They whine constantly and keep the whole household awake. If this occurs, you may try speaking reassuringly to the puppy. Whether or not this works, be prepared to persevere. It doesn't take all that long to break in a new puppy. After three or four days, it will probably sleep quietly all night long.

A Private Spot and Furniture

If you decide not to use a crate, your beagle will still need a private spot in your house to which you can send it when you don't want it underfoot and where it can spend the night. Dogs don't have a preference for any particular spot. They accept the space you assign them. You can't, however, keep changing the dog's spot in the house. Dogs are creatures of habit and don't follow if you move their space from here to there.

There are varied opinions about the best location. People have used a large, well-ventilated kitchen closet, a corner in the den, or the space between two pieces of furniture, like a bookcase and a bench. Any of these is all right with the beagle, as long as it can be close to its human friends. It wouldn't like a space in a room that people don't use much.

The most important consideration is that the dog's crate or private spot be free of drafts and moisture. Further, the spot should be easy to

Basic Rules of Beagle Care

clean, so cover it with an old blanket. However, this lining should not be too hard, because this would promote calluses on the dog's skin. You need to protect the dog's pressure points, which are the hock joints, the elbows, and the pasterns.

Don't put the dog's space too close to a stove or heat outlet. I know of a beagle that had almost constant problems with an earache because it had the habit of lying on the grate of the central heating system. Set it up so the dog will be comfortably warm but not so hot that the difference between inside and outside temperatures is excessive. Bear in mind that dogs generally prefer cooler temperatures than do human beings.

Furniture for the dog's spot can be varied. You can use a basket, of which there are a variety on the market. The traditional wicker basket looks quite cozy. Put a few blankets inside, and it makes a fine resting place.

A disadvantage of wicker baskets is that beagles (and various other breeds) like to chew on them, so that it doesn't take long before the sides are gnawed to bits and only the bottom remains. You can solve this problem in part by wrapping a thin piece of wire around the rim of the basket. Dogs hate the taste of metal, and if they can't chew on the rim, they usually won't chew on the rest of the basket, either. Remember: *never* permit your beagle to chew on anything other than hard rubber toys, rawhide "bones," and the like. Try to catch transgressions in the act and scold the puppy promptly.

A second disadvantage of wicker baskets is that they are hard to clean properly. All kinds of dirt can accumulate between the reeds. The best way to clean them is to take a hard brush with long bristles and scrub away!

It may prove simpler to get a hard plastic basket. Hard plastic is usually too tough for the beagle to get its teeth into. Cleaning it is simple with soft soap. The disadvantage of a plastic basket is that it doesn't permit evaporation of moisture. If you put a thin pillow in it, the pillow will be moist on the bottom after only a single night of use. The best lining is a pure woolen blanket. You can promote evaporation by drilling a few small holes in the bottom of the basket and around the sides, just above the bottom. This creates a small flow of air to carry moisture away.

It is best to avoid baskets made of styrofoam. They are hard to clean and easy to chew on. Dogs can get an intestinal blockage from pieces gnawed from them.

If you want to make your beagle really happy, give it a spot up off the floor, where it can see more of the activity around it. Provide space on a bench or an old chair. An old reclining chair is ideal. You can cover it with an old blanket, or you can get one of the modern polyester blankets that look like sheep fur. These are simple to launder.

The Doghouse

You may decide to house the beagle outdoors in its own doghouse. A reason for this decision could be lack of space inside your home or a desire to keep the beagle from constantly being underfoot.

I see no objection to a doghouse, provided you can protect your beagle from moisture, drafts, and cold. Cold should not be a serious concern. Beagles can stand relatively low temperatures because they grow a new, thick coat of fur in the fall. You should, however, do everything you can to keep dogs warm at all times.

The floor of the doghouse should be made of wood that is easily cleaned and sanitized. It should be at least 1¼ inch (3 cm) thick. Raise it off the ground at least 4 inches (10 cm) with wooden props to permit proper ventilation.

To get the right dimensions for the doghouse, measure your beagle. The two measurements you need most are height at the withers (the high point of the shoulders) and length, measured between the base of the tail and the withers.

The height of the doghouse should be at least one-and-a-half times the height of your beagle at the withers. The depth should be at least one-and-a-half times your dog's length.

Along one side of the doghouse, build a corridor that runs the length of the house. At the back, make a doorway from the corridor into the rest of

The doghouse. Hinging the roof panels facilitates cleaning and airing.

The Run

To build a run, provide floor space of at least 24 square feet (7 m²); the width should be about 1 yard (approximately 1 m) or more. Beagles can move freely inside this space, but there's nothing wrong with providing additional room.

Be sure the floor isn't moist. You have a choice of several floorings: gravel, dry sand, a grass mat, tile, or concrete. However, the flooring must be cleansed and disinfected, so it is best to choose a substance that is impervious to water.

At least one of the sides of the run should be made of chain link fencing with a mesh size of 2 inches (5 cm). A trellis is all right, but it is more difficult to construct. You can build a kennel in the space between three walls, but it's more pleasant for the dog to have a free run.

The run should be connected to the doghouse. Don't make the doghouse smaller, though, because of the run.

Pay attention to the direction of the sun. Beagles love to sunbathe, preferably on a raised platform. When it gets too hot, however, they seek protection in the shade. You should orient the run so that the beagle can find both sun and shade.

the house; make the doorway as wide as the corridor. The rest of the doghouse is the beagle's sleeping quarters, which will measure one "dog height" by one-and-one-half "dog lengths."

Make the front of the house higher than the rear, so water can run off the roof. Let the roof project over the front of the house by about 8 inches (20 cm) or more. At the sides and the rear, it should project at least 2 inches (5 cm). The roof must be moisture proof. Make it removable for easier cleaning of the doghouse.

Feel free to make the floor space of the house larger if you like. You must certainly do this if the house should hold more than one beagle. The height can remain the same.

If you like, you can also build a window into the front of the house. Remember, however, that most dogs look out by pressing their snouts against the glass, so that the window quickly becomes dirty.

I suggest you get a self-closing door for the doghouse, which you can buy in a pet store. The door is easy to install and helps keep the house free from drafts. Cover the floor with old blankets, sheets, or the like.

Boarding Kennels

When you go on vacation without your beagle, you must plan ahead. You can leave the dog with family, friends, or neighbors or ask someone to dog-sit. If that doesn't work, you must find a boarding kennel. Not all of these are equally good, so get a recommendation from fellow members of the beagle club or from your veterinarians, who may even operate a kennel themselves.

Good kennels are booked early, so count on making reservations for your dog before you make reservations for your own trip. You may have to book space for your dog in November or December if you want to go on vacation in July or August.

Basic Rules of Beagle Care

Reputable kennels insist that your beagle's vaccinations be current. Check with the kennel about what vaccinations are required and with your veterinarian to be sure the vaccinations you have are current. Also be sure your dog is free of fleas and other parasites—the kennel doesn't want an infestation.

When you take your beagle to the kennel, ask the person in charge if you may take along a basket or another familiar piece of furniture. Toys and other equipment of that type are better left at home. They are too easily lost.

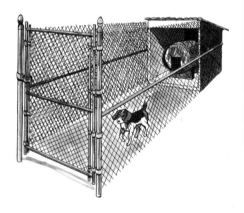

The run with shelter makes an ideal combination for a beagle. It provides an escape-proof doghouse and a safe place for exercise.

Check ahead to see what type of feed they use at the kennel. You may even want to take along a good supply of your beagle's favorite food if you think there may be any trouble with eating.

Even so, your beagle may eat little or nothing while it is at the kennel. Beagles are devoted pets and they easily become homesick. Your dog may look starved, wild, and nervous when you see it again. Don't blame the kennel operator. If you selected the kennel wisely, the operator will have done the best possible under the circumstances.

Traveling with your Beagle

If your dog goes along on vacation, make sure that the hotels and motels you book accept dogs (consult a travel guide or phone in advance). Take along a folding kennel. This is constructed so that it can fit into a small space, and you'll be able to put it into your car.

Some states and most foreign countries require vaccination before they allow your dog to enter. Some even require a quarantine, in which case you'd better not plan to take your dog. Be sure to get this type of information ahead of time. Call your veterinarian, your travel agent, or the consulate of the country you plan to visit.

Take along your beagle's regular feeding dishes, sleeping basket, blanket, collar and leash, comb and brush, and a first-aid kit. Make sure you'll be able to get your dog's familiar food en route. Check with the travel agent in case of doubt. If the agent doesn't know, write to the manufacturer of the product you use.

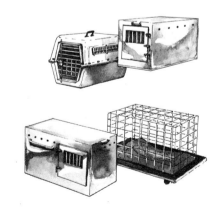

Various traveling containers. One of these is a good investment if you and your pet will be using public transportation.

Basic Rules of Beagle Care

Staying Alone—the Security Room

There will doubtlessly be times when a young or adult beagle must stay at home alone. It may happen every day. Therefore, you should train your beagle from the first day to be locked into a secure room where it can't do too much damage and where it will not injure itself. The first day, put the dog into the security room along with a familiar basket and toys. Start with about 10 minutes of solitude, and keep quiet during that time. If your beagle thinks you're around, it will spend all its energy to get to you as quickly as possible. Lengthen the time of solitude by several minutes on successive days until the dog can remain quiet for an entire hour.

The first few days you'll hear howls and cries, but if you make confinement a regular thing, your beagle will accept it, not as a punishment, but as a regular part of the daily routine. It will learn to amuse itself if you provide a hard rubber ball or a nylon bone.

Of course, don't leave a rug or carpet in the security room. The flooring should be tile or wood, so that you can easily clean feces and urine. If there are curtains, be sure they are high off the ground, so the dog can't reach them. Also, don't keep a bookcase with books in the room, because beagles love to play with and tear at books and magazines. I learned that lesson from bitter experience!

Toys—Good and Bad

It pays to buy proper toys for your beagle. Veterinarians tell endless stories about strange objects they have removed from the stomachs of dogs, including stones, balls, needles, nails, corks, and rubber bands. As you may suspect, some of these objects can cause all sorts of damage.

Dogs don't swallow objects because they're hungry. They do it in the course of play. You can avoid this problem by furnishing entertaining and safe toys. Many beagles love to play with a ball, but make it a proper ball. Small balls, like Ping-Pong balls and marbles, are not recommended because they can be swallowed and choke the dog. Don't get a ball that your beagle can bite through, and don't get one that doesn't bounce.

Squeaking toys are also not recommended. Even if the squeaking doesn't drive you crazy, they can be dangerous. Your beagle can quickly gnaw apart the toy so that the squeaker drops out, and in nine out of ten cases the beagle will swallow it. Surgery is generally the only solution!

Many synthetic materials are dangerous, as are toys made of wood that splinters easily. Rubber balls and rubber bones are suitable only if your beagle just plays with them. If it starts biting and chewing on them, take them away. Rubber is not digestible and can cause intestinal upsets.

Imitation bones made of rawhide and similar toys are ideal, as are artificial bones, balls, and rings of hard nylon (but don't get those coated with chocolate).

I recommend that you give proper toys to puppies when they are quite young. It strengthens their teeth and exercises their chewing muscles.

An old shoe has been used as a dog toy for ages, but I don't recommend this. Tanned leather doesn't dissolve well in the stomach, and if your beagle swallows pieces of any size, they can cause blockage of the intestines. Further, you are setting up a potentially confusing situation, since your puppy will not understand the difference between an old slipper and your brand new one! I advise against letting your beagle play with leather shoes and slippers.

Beagles are very responsive, naturally curious, and wonderful companions. They are always ready for a romp!

Basic Rules of Beagle Care

Necessary Equipment

When you acquire a beagle, you may be tempted by all the fancy equipment offered in the pet store. Think through your needs calmly, and buy only what you find useful. Here is a list of helpful or necessary items.

• A lined leather or soft nylon collar is useful, especially if your puppy is a bit wild. In fact, I recommend a harness for such cases.

• A leash of normal length—about 6 feet (2 m) —is good to use when you take the beagle for a walk. Since puppies love to gnaw at anything resembling leather, consider getting a leash with a short section of chain links at the end. At any rate, do what you can to keep the puppy from gnawing on the leash; it's not good for the dog.

• Also get a long or reel leash, the kind with a spring that automatically rolls up. It helps your dog let off extra energy when you go for a walk, and it is also very handy for training purposes.

• A muzzle may be legally required in areas where there is a rabies outbreak. It is also handy when you go visiting, when you go to the veterinarian, or if you take a trip. Beagles are not known as biters, but generally it's best not to take risks.

• Get two dishes, one for food and one for water. Since beagles are lop-eared, get dishes that narrow toward the top. Get heavy models that can't be upset or pushed away easily. You can minimize having dishes pushed around too much by gluing a strip of rubber on the bottom.

The choke collar (top, left), formed by slipping one ring through the other and attaching the leash, is used for training. The simple nylon or leather collar (top, right) is for general use. The harness (bottom) may be needed for training particularly stubborn dogs.

Top: While being posed, this handsome beagle kept a keen eye on the photographer. Bottom: Beagles are shown in two classes: "not exceeding 13 inches" and "over 13 inches but not exceeding 15 inches." Championship points are awarded in both divisions.

The long or reel leash enables you to adjust the free play when walking your beagle.

Basic Rules of Beagle Care

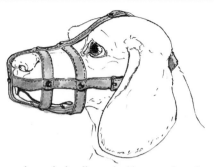

A muzzle may be legally required in areas where there is a rabies outbreak.

- A metal comb and a brush are also important (see page 22). Also get a narrow-toothed "louse comb" (see page 27). Use brushes with natural bristles. I also recommend a grooming glove.
- Get tweezers and a good brand of flea powder.
- Get spray foam cleaner at your pet store. This can serve as a waterless bath. It can provide protection against fleas and other pests. The same is true of a dry shampoo, which I personally like to use when beagles are still quite small.
- A protective spray for the paws can come in quite handy, especially if you take your beagle for a walk in the woods in winter, with snow on the ground. The spray protects against road salts, and it keeps the pads from becoming cracked and sore.

Dog bowls of different shapes and sizes.

- A dependable brand of flea collar is recommended to keep away all types of vermin, such as fleas, mites, and ticks. Some types can protect the dog for two months, or even up to four or six months.
- Get disinfectants that destroy all types of pathogens. You need one product that can be used safely on the beagle itself and another to use on the sleeping box or basket, doghouse, and run.
- A repellent spray is a good defense when young puppies forget their toilet training. The spray can help wipe out the dirty traces of misplaced feces or urine. To prevent more damage, you can spray in house corners and entryways and on furniture, carpet, certain trees and bushes, and flowers, among other places.
- Also important are protective panties made of heavy material to put on a female in heat; they are available in any pet store. This keeps your carpet, furniture, and other household goods from becoming soiled. They come in different sizes; ask your veterinarian for advice.
- Rubber massage brushes and/or rubber grooming gloves are essential for grooming your short-haired beagle.
- Get a small leather pocket (or something similar—various models are available) that attaches to the collar. In it you can put your address and telephone number as well as a couple of quarters. That way, if your beagle is lost, the finder can easily notify you. You can also obtain metal address tags in pet stores. These may also be attached to the collar.

Beagles and Children

Beagles are affectionate and adore children. They are wonderful companions, gentle, playful, and even-tempered. In fact, beagles are also friendly to other pets, including other dogs and even cats. I once knew a beagle that daily licked clean the ears of a cat in the household; the cat, in turn, groomed the beagle!

On the other hand, beagles are spirited dogs, and if they get into conflict with a child, the child

Basic Rules of Beagle Care

Beagles are wonderful companions, gentle, playful and even-tempered. They are affectionate and adore children.

may not be able to hold its own. Beagles love to play with children and may even take the role of protector; this doesn't mean that children can treat beagles any way they like. Teach your children not to abuse or threaten your family pet. Also, teach them to recognize when the beagle wants to be left alone and when it invites play. Beagles often make such invitations, but there are moments when they really want to be alone and left in peace.

For that reason, it's important for you to keep an eye on the situation when a beagle and a child play together. My point is this: Be sure to teach your children to treat your dog properly.

If you expect a new baby, give your beagle extra attention so that it doesn't feel its position in the family is threatened. When the baby comes, let the beagle be with you when you tend the child. Let the beagle smell the baby, and meanwhile speak to the dog gently and kindly. Try to avoid ordering the beagle away when you're with the baby. This just makes the beagle insecure about the "intruder" in the family.

Grooming

Washing

Beagles have a different concept of cleanliness than you do. They may lick parts of their bodies from time to time, but they don't go much further in taking care of themselves. As a result, you will have to turn your hand to grooming. Basically, you need to brush the dog regularly, comb it, and wash it now and then.

Dogs secrete sebum, a type of natural lubricant that keeps the hair and skin supple. When you wash your beagle, the sebum is dissolved and rinsed away. Since the sebum will soon return, no harm is done. Nevertheless, it is best not to wash the beagle at all until there is a good reason for it.

A good time for a bath is when your pet decides to take a mud bath, rolls in rotting leaves, or gets manure on its fur. You don't want to get dirt and stench in the house, so a bath is the only solution. You can also wash the dog if it is shedding. If you use a lot of water, comfortably hot, you'll help loosen the hairs. Then, when you brush the beagle while the fur dries, you'll brush out most of the hair, shortening the shedding time.

Use only a shampoo made especially for short-haired dogs. You'll find many good brands at the pet store that remove a minimum amount of sebum from the hair. If your beagle has problems with its coat, ask your veterinarian for a medicated shampoo that can help. Many dog shampoos contain an insecticide that removes fleas, ticks, and other vermin during the bath.

Generally, beagles like the bath. They enjoy swimming, after all. Some beagles hate getting water in their ear canal, however. You'll get a hint of this if you see the dog constantly shake its head. So put a good wad of cotton balls in the ears before you start.

Then wet the dog's whole body with lukewarm water. The best place to work is on a rubber mat in the bathtub. When the beagle is wet all over, massage some shampoo through the hairs and onto the skin. Take your time, so that the shampoo penetrates as deeply as possible. Then, thoroughly rinse away the shampoo. Then, shampoo a second time. As you rub it in, you'll probably get a good foam, which helps the shampoo penetrate even better. Really take your time with the second round, especially if there is an insecticide in the shampoo. To be effective against fleas and other vermin, the shampoo has to stay on the dog at least 10 minutes. Again rinse—thoroughly. Don't skimp on water. You don't want to leave shampoo on your beagle. If shampoo dries on the fur, it can cause the hair to rub off, causing a skin irritation or infection.

Now take the cotton out of the ears and dry the dog. You can use an ordinary hand-held blow dryer. Be sure to brush the coat while you dry it. Brush lightly in the direction in which the hairs grow so that the hair drops down smoothly and doesn't become matted. (Matting isn't usually a problem with beagles.) Brush one area of coat at a time. When you've covered the whole dog, go over the fur with a comb to detect any small remaining snarls. Loosen these carefully.

Brushing

Generally, your beagle requires a bath only once or twice a year, but a good brushing is a frequent requirement. After a few sessions, your beagle will be used to it; it will pull back its hind legs and lie like a prince while it enjoys the grooming. Don't be fooled because your beagle's coat generally looks neat; a brushing is absolutely necessary. It helps remove any loose hair.

You can obtain a special rubber brush made for short-haired dogs. Pull this through the fur several times, and you'll collect a good number of loose hairs. Brushing also massages the skin, loosening scaly skin. The scales work their way through the hair and rest on top of the coat, making it look dusty. Just leave the dusty scales there. In a half-hour's time, the dog will have shaken off a good many of them. After that, remove the rest with a damp washcloth. If you want to do a really professional job, use a grooming glove or a chamois cloth.

Always brush from the neck across the back to the tail in strong strokes. Then brush from the

Grooming

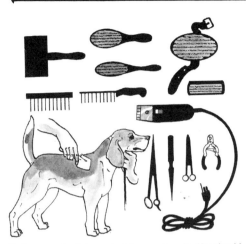

Daily grooming is important for your beagle. You should use a narrow-toothed comb and then brush with natural bristles. After a thorough combing—*with* the lay of fur—the beagle should be brushed just as thoroughly.

neck across the shoulders and along the front legs, downward, and again from the neck along the flanks, acrosss the hip, and downward along the rear legs.

Care of the Teeth

A few weeks after whelping, puppies get their baby teeth. Several months later, these are exchanged for permanent teeth. Generally this causes no problems, but in a rare case, the eyeteeth (canine teeth) don't drop out. You'll notice sharp, pointed baby teeth next to or behind the permanent eyeteeth. The baby teeth must be removed, or they will push the permanent teeth from their place. Take your young beagle to the veterinarian and have the old eyeteeth removed if they persist beyond the ninth month of life.

Generally, you needn't expect trouble with teeth until your beagle reaches one-and-a-half to two years of age. After that, you may start noticing

plaque, a soft layer of dirt formed by decaying food, bacteria, and saliva. At first it is rather white, but soon the color changes to yellow. Most plaque starts at the gum line, then spreads over the enamel of the tooth. If not removed, plaque may create cornice-like extensions overhanging adjacent teeth but not actually covering them.

Plaque is easy to remove. Brush the teeth from time to time, and the plaque disappears. You can use a regular toothbrush and toothpaste. Don't use an abrasive tooth cleanser. This removes the plaque all right, but also causes slight damage to the enamel.

Your beagle needs to learn at a young age that its teeth are going to be brushed at times. If you don't get it accustomed to this procedure, you'll always have your hands full trying to get the dog to sit still and keep its mouth open.

Don't worry too much about caries (cavities). They don't often occur in dogs—unlike the situation in humans.

Our saliva contains an enzyme that converts starches to sugar. In addition, we ingest a great deal of sugar in candy, cake, and soft drinks. As a result, we frequently have sugar residues in our mouth. Bacteria found in the mouth convert the sugar to acid, which attacks the enamel and soon produces cavities.

Dogs, in contrast, don't have the enzyme that converts carbohydrates to sugar, so that a dog's mouth usually has little or no sugar in it. Nowadays, you do see some beagles with cavities. This indicates they are being fed sweets or are being given regular feed with sugar in it.

Still, I'd worry more about plaque, which may soon become mixed with calcium and other substances to form an insoluble whole (dental calculus). This can result in thick layers of deposits that build up to a millimeter or more in all too many cases.

The build up of dental calculus can lead to three types of problems. First, it causes an unpleasant smell. Second, the rough surface of the deposit chafes the lips and tongue. In the end, the deposits can become so large that they are pushed between the gum and the base of the tooth and ultimately cause infections in the roots of the teeth. The teeth are loosened, exert painful pressure on the gums, and ultimately fall out.

You can retard plaque deposits on the teeth by providing the right kind of feed. Many people say that hard food scours away part of these deposits, and this is true. I also recommend giving your beagle a hard rawhide or nylon bone (not a chocolate-coated one, however!) to chew on.

Further, you can prevent tooth deposits by regularly brushing your beagle's teeth. If they still get deposits, take your dog to the veterinarian. Some veterinarians have a complete collection of dental apparatus; others cooperate with a dentist. If your dog has loose or badly decayed teeth, they should be pulled so that they don't cause further trouble.

Foot Care

Many dogs have a lot of hair growing between the toes, although this is a lesser problem in beagles. Still, check your beagle to make sure that hair growth there isn't excessive because this can make dogs quite uncomfortable. The toes are bent apart, and the usual, beautiful, round, closed foot becomes a splayfoot, interfering with walking and standing. So keep an eye on those hairs between the toes and clip them if necessary. Don't go so far as to shave them off completely because a certain amount of hair is good protection for the skin.

Also check for hair between the foot pads. This hair can also cause problems—for instance if the dog steps into a discarded piece of chewing gum. When the gum sticks to obects as the dog walks and pulls on the hair, the dog is in pain. You can prevent this whole scenario by keeping the pad hairs short. This also helps prevent trouble in the winter, when snow and ice can stick to the pad hairs, making the foot a clump of ice. So keep a sharp eye on your dog's pads in freezing weather.

Your dog can get sore pads from small cracks that develop there. As long as the cracks stay shallow, they should be considered normal, but if they become deep, you must take action. You don't want your dog to limp or go lame. Start by rub-

bing the pads with a good baby salve, cod-liver oil salve, or any salve with a glycerine base. If this doesn't bring relief in a day or two, consult a veterinarian. In any case, I suggest you put socks on the sore feet (available at your local pet store) to keep the pad free from dirt until the wounds have healed.

Care of the Nails

Beagles that walk on hard surfaces keep wearing down their nails so that they never need to be cut. If you keep your beagle on soft surfaces or don't let it exercise much, the nails tend to grow too long. I have seen nails that have grown so long that they curve and grow back into the skin, causing a serious infection. Don't let the nails grow to that point; clip them if necessary.

Nail clipping isn't hard, particularly if you train your beagle to tolerate it at an early age. Take a strong pair of clippers—available commercially in several models—and trim a piece of the nail. It's very simple.

Just don't clip too deeply. The nail grows around a tiny cone of connective tissue that con-

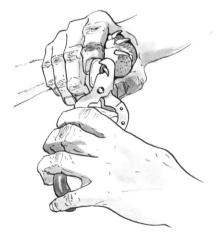

Clipping nails. Several types of clippers are available. The guillotine-type, shown here, works well.

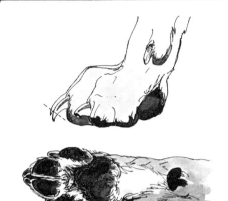

Cut the nail at an angle toward the base of the paw, taking care not to cut into the quick.

tains blood vessels and nerves. When you cut too deeply, you clip off the tip of this sensitive tissue. The dog will jump up in pain, and blood may spurt from the wound. Naturally, your dog will never again sit still for another nail clipping.

The lesson is clear: Never clip into the live part of the nail. If the nails are white and transparent, it is generally easy to see where the live part starts. Tissue with capillaries shows with a bluish tinge. But if the nails are black or dark, you won't be able to see these signs and you will have to use your good judgment. Some people quickly develop a sense of where to cut and seldom make a mistake. Others err repeatedly.

I advise that you cut only up to the point where the cut nail is just above the ground when the dog stands upright normally. Then you can round off the cut end neatly with a file so that there are no rough edges.

If you do tap blood, let the wound bleed for a little while. Then press the wound closed with a bandage. When the bleeding stops, put some nonstinging iodine on the wound. If you don't trust yourself to do the nail trimming right, let a professional do it for you.

There is one instance in which you shouldn't hesitate to take prompt action yourself, that is when your beagle just about tears out a nail during a fast run or rough play. If you don't attend to a loose nail, it will cause your beagle recurring pain and trouble. So take the loose nail tightly in your fingers and pull it out with a quick motion. Then cover the wound with a clean, sterile piece of surgical gauze, and treat it with a disinfecting wound powder. When the wound is completely dry, you can let the dog go.

If the nail is completely torn out, it does not grow back although a short stump may develop. You can file this down from time to time to keep it nice and round. This job is really simple.

The Ears

Beagles and many other hunting hounds have hanging or "flap ears" that protect the ear canal against dust and dirt. This is an advantage in the hunt, when dogs have to chase after prey across dusty and muddy terrain.

The ear flaps should be washed from time to time, perhaps at the same time as an overall bath. It is amazing how much dirt can accumulate along the edges. This dirt is a mixture of wax, dust,

Cleaning the ear with a cotton swab. *Do not probe into the ear canal.*

sand, and hairs. If soap and water don't get rid of it, use cotton balls or swabs moistened with a little rubbing alcohol. Be very gentle. Also, be aware that this treatment removes all body fats. So follow it up with an application of baby oil. After a thorough cleaning, the ears may appear quite bald.

Note: Oil is harmful to the ear canal; don't permit any oily substance to enter it.

A problem can arise if a beagle comes down with an ear infection that causes it to scratch its ears hard or shake them against a chair, table leg, wall, or cupboard. This can cause subcutaneous bleeding, which needs to be relieved by the veterinarian—an operation that is not at all simple. Naturally, prevention is better than having to cure. If you see your beagle shake its ears against the furniture, take a close look and be sure the dog doesn't have an ear infection.

Hair in the Ear Canal

The ear canal is lined with skin that can grow hair, particularly near the opening. Some breeds are especially hairy and experience frequent problems with hair in the ears. This is not the case with beagles, but I still recommend checking the ear occasionally. Too much hair can keep the ear canal from being properly ventilated, which can foster a number of bacterial infections.

If you see too much hair growth, pull it out carefully with a pair of tweezers. Beagles don't like people messing with their ears, so do the job with kindness and gentleness. Once again, train your dog to tolerate the process while it is still quite young.

Cleaning the Ear Canal

If your beagle is healthy and its ear is functioning properly, you never (or hardly ever) have to clean out the ear canal. It tends to be self-cleaning. You should still inspect the canal, however.

Start by checking if there is ear wax and, if so, how much. Notice the color. If it is light to dark brown, all is well. Use your sense of smell. If there's a stench, suspect an ear infection. Rub the base of the ear directly behind the juncture with the head. If you hear "sloshing," there is an excess

of exudates and perhaps an infection. At the least indication of an ear infection, immediately consult your veterinarian. If you are sure that nothing serious is wrong, continue cleaning the ears. Use an otic solution, which you can obtain from your veterinarian.

Ear Mites

A type of mite *(Otodectes cynotis)* lives in the dog's ear canal. This ear mite causes an ear infection, which can be detected by excessive wax that is generally dark brown to black in color. The consistency of the wax generally turns grainy. The infection itches and causes the dog to scratch. As the infection progresses, your beagle will be in pain. It will hold its head at an angle and shake its ears. Depend on your veterinarian to get rid of this pest.

Fleas

Dog fleas are 0.08–0.12 inch (2–3 mm) in size, with the females somewhat larger than the males. They are reddish brown and have six legs.

Fleas mainly infest the neck, the back, the legs, and the base of the tail. They bite the dog, causing

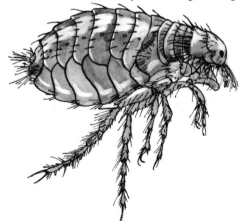

Fleas can cause your beagle to scratch itself almost incessantly. They also serve as intermediate hosts for tapeworms.

26

an itch. The dog reacts by scratching, biting, and chafing at the itch. A heavy infestation can greatly weaken the dog. It becomes thin and suffers from anemia. Young dogs can even die from a bad infestation. Furthermore, fleas can serve as intermediate hosts for tapeworms.

Don't delay treatment. As soon as you notice fleas, wash your beagle thoroughly with an antiparasitic shampoo. Then treat it with flea powder, which is available at the pet store in several brands.

Flea larvae are quite sensitive to moisture, so it helps to scrub the house thoroughly with an insecticide dissolved in water. Pay close attention to cracks and seams in the floor and to wall-to-wall carpets.

Put a flea collar on the beagle, especially in the summer months. If it continues to scratch itself, look for another cause. Perhaps there is something in the feed that causes a skin irritation.

Lice

Although dogs don't often get lice, two types can cause an infestation. One is the sucking louse, which is 0.04–0.08 inch (1–2 mm) in size and lives on skin scales and blood. The second type is the biting (or blood louse), which is somewhat

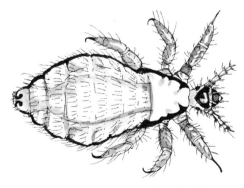

Lice will also cause frequent scratching. Look for egg clusters if you suspect lice.

larger. It has a pointed mouthpiece used to drill into the skin and suck blood. The nits, or lice eggs, are glued to dog hairs.

Lice irritate the skin, causing your beagle to rub against objects and scratch itself. You can find them most frequently on the neck. Lice that infest dogs are never a danger to humans.

Fight lice as soon as you see them. Use a nit comb and a flea collar for starters. Then ask the veterinarian for further advice.

Ticks

Ticks are arachnids. Males are about 0.06–0.08 inch (1½–2 mm) long and reddish brown or black in color. Females are 0.16 inch (4 mm) long and yellowish red.

Ticks hide in low bushes. When a beagle walks by, they drop down, especially during the summer months. They attach themselves to the skin and suck blood. In a few days, the body of the tick grows to the size of a pea and becomes bluish gray.

Keep an eye open for ticks when you stroke your beagle and when you groom it, which you ought to do daily, especially in summer.

A tick clamps its mouthpiece into the skin of the dog and is therefore difficult to remove. If you try to pull off the tick, the head of the tick remains and can quickly cause an infection that is quite painful to the dog. The best way to remove a tick is to use alcohol or acetone. Place one drop on the tick's head. Wait a moment, and then you can lift

A tick, before feeding (right) and after feeding (left).

the pest from the dog's skin with a pair of tweezers. Do not twist. Use firm and constant upward pressure. Disinfect the place where the tick was attached. Then, drop the tick into a saucer of alcohol and leave it there for several hours.

Note: Dog ticks can transmit Rocky Mountain spotted fever—a dangerous disease characterized by muscular pains, high fever, and skin eruptions. Since the disease is endemic throughout North America, anyone who comes in contact with animals and displays these symptoms should see a physician immediately.

The Proper Diet

The digestive system of the dog is typical of carnivores. The overall length of the digestive tract is shorter (proportionately) than that of humans and much shorter than that of cattle and other animals that chew their cud. A canine's teeth are adapted for tearing the flesh of prey and are hardly useful for chewing or grinding grains and vegetables.

Foods for dogs can be split into two groups: those of animal origin and those of plant origin. The latter, which only indirectly form part of the dog's diet in nature, leave the digestive system largely unused if not suitably processed.

Meat

Some people believe that since dogs are carnivores, they should be fed only meat. That's an oversimplification, and it ignores advances in modern nutrition. The modern concept is based on the body's need for protein, carbohydrates, fat, vitamins, and minerals.

Meat is rich in protein and fat, both of which can also be found in foods of plant origin. However, meat is low or lacking in certain of the other basic nutritional elements. So, we have to add sources of carbohydrate to the diet, as well as some essential minerals and vitamins.

Let's take a closer look at various kinds of meat.

Beef is excellent for dogs and has a biologic rating (i.e., the index indicating the presence of essential amino acids) of 76.

Mutton and goat meat are also first rate.

Horse meat is a good source, but some dogs are allergic to it. The allergies are manifested by red skin and an itch.

Pork is excellent, with a biologic rating of 79, higher than beef. Still, it isn't fed to dogs often because it can cause allergic reactions. It also poses a risk from pseudorabies (Aujeszky's disease), a viral infection that is absolutely fatal to dogs. The risk of infection (and of trichinosis) can be eliminated by thorough cooking.

Poultry is a good protein source but contains very little of the other essential elements for dogs. Furthermore, the small bones tend to splinter, and the sharp points can easily damage a dog's gullet.

Veal, like all meat of young animals, is not so good. It has too few minerals, among other deficiencies.

Animal meal is prepared from animal carrion, which is unfit for human consumption. It is made safe for animal feed by a lengthy heating process. Animal meal is ground and commercially enriched as a complete, dry dog food.

Dried meat is prepared under high temperatures and is therefore generally low in vitamins. It can be a good source of protein and minerals, however.

Bones are a controversial item in the dog diet. Soft veal bones and cartilage are fine; soft bones can be gnawed to your beagle's content and eaten whole. They provide a good source of calcium and phosphorus. I recommend in particular the soft shoulder bones of veal.

The nutritional value of harder bones is minimal. They offer the benefit of helping keep teeth free of plaque but also tend to wear them down. Good, safe gnawing can be provided in the form of beef and rawhide that has been pressed together for the purpose.

Never feed bones from poultry and swine. They contain up to 80% calcium, which causes them to splinter easily.

Other Protein Sources

Fish is an excellent source of protein and carries a higher biologic rating than red meat (at least a value of 80). It is also a good source of unsaturated fat and makes for good variety. Always boil freshwater fish to inactivate an element that would otherwise destroy vitamin B_1. Don't feed smoked and salted fish. Naturally, be on guard against bones; they should be carefully removed from your beagle's rations.

I particularly recommend *hake* (dried cod), which contains 71% protein. It is strengthening and nourishing if fed occasionally, and it is convenient, as it can be handled dry. So is *fish meal,* which is prepared commercially in the same way as animal meal.

Milk is especially essential for young dogs. It is an excellent source of protein as well as a well-balanced source of calcium and phosphorus. It's fine to give your dog a daily serving of milk, but don't feed only milk. Also, don't neglect to supply drinking water. Most dogs like milk better than water and easily drink more of it than is good for them.

Don't worry about talk that milk causes ulcerated eyes. There is no truth to that tale!

Older animals may have problems with milk, but if you provide milk regularly your dog will generally remain accustomed to it. The issue is whether the dog produces enough of the enzyme lactase, which digests milk sugar (lactose). As the dog ages, it tends to produce less lactase. If you run into problems with diarrhea, feed less milk or replace it with buttermilk, which is also very healthy for dogs.

Eggs are probably the best available source of protein. The biologic rating of chicken eggs, for example, is a high 96. Always boil eggs for three minutes or so, to inactivate avidin and antitrypsin. Avidin counteracts biotin (vitamin H) and antitrypsin counteracts trypsin, a digestive enzyme. Raw eggs are 60% digestible, and boiled eggs are 90% digestible.

Eggs are especially important for young dogs, and even an older dog can make use of an occasional egg in the diet for extra strength. Too many eggs, however, can increase the risk of arteriosclerosis in dogs, just as in humans. Soft-boiled eggs are excellent to keep stud (male) dogs in prime breeding condition. Eggs also serve to strengthen dogs weakened by sickness or dogs with a poor coat.

Cheese provides a good source of protein and fat, but it should be fed to dogs only if prepared from milk without additives. Feed only fresh cheese, and be sure to remove any plastic rind. Never feed moldy cheese.

Cheese is expensive and recommended mainly when your dog is eating poorly or is recovering from illness.

Carbohydrates

Dogs depend principally on foods of vegetable origin for their carbohydrates. However, the dog's natural digestive organs can't break down the cell walls of plants, so that unprocessed vegetables, grains, and the like are almost indigestible. You need to adapt them to your beagle's needs: chop them fine, grind them, or cook them.

Grains, as indicated, are indigestible for dogs as whole grain. The food value inside the grains must be released by processing. When ground into flour, they become quite digestible, however, and grains like corn make up a good part of commercial dog food. A number of other products furnish digestible grains.

Bread, contrary to popular belief, may be fed to your beagle. Whole-wheat bread is preferable to white bread, although it can be mildly laxative. Whole wheat contains all the germ and hulls of whole grain and is therefore richer in vitamin B, which more than makes up for its slightly lower digestibility. Bread, especially white bread, can cause intestinal congestion, more so when it is fresh. Always feed dogs stale (but not moldy) bread.

Dog biscuits come in two forms—with or without meat. Most brands are made with poor-quality meat (mostly cracklings), which isn't tolerated too well by dogs and can in some instances cause a bad case of diarrhea. Never depend totally on dog biscuits to feed your beagle.

Cookies baked for human consumption should not be considered a treat for dogs. Better to give your beagle dog biscuits, suitable bones, and other proper treats.

Cooked cereals generally constitute the main food given puppies and very young dogs. It's fine to use commercially prepared cereals intended for children. Some are made of grain mixes, including wheat, buckwheat, and barley.

The Proper Diet

Rice, especially whole-grain rice, is a good source of carbohydrates, provided it is well cooked. Check the stools of your beagle for signs that rice is passing through its system undigested (but don't confuse rice with segments of tapeworm—see page 52. If there is a problem, rice probably isn't right for your beagle.

Peas and beans are another good source of carbohydrates, but they have to be cooked until completely done and then thoroughly mashed. Even then, some dogs don't handle these legumes too well. If tolerated, they can be a partial source of protein as well as carbohydrates. Peas carry a biologic rating of 48 and beans, 38.

Soy pellets are a good protein source (with a biologic rating of 75) and a good source of roughage. The pellets are specially treated with superheated steam under pressure to make them more digestible.

Potatoes are a potential source of carbohydrates that is questioned by some authorities (the biologic rating is 71). One of the problems with potatoes is that they can ferment in the stomach. However, the disadvantages of potatoes in the diet of your beagle can be overcome if you're willing to take some precautions.

First, thinly peel the potatoes and take out all the eyes. These can cause intestinal cramps. Then, boil the potatoes until they are thoroughly cooked, and puree them. This improves the digestibility. When you boil potatoes, you can add a bit of salt to the water—about the same amount as you would use when preparing potatoes for yourself.

Other Vegetables should always be boiled as little as possible, in as little water as possible. I provide them staight from the pan between other elements of the meal. You can use almost any kind of vegetable. Vegetables generally contain a good amount of vitamins and minerals.

Fats and Oils

Fats and oils are essential to the dog's diet even though too much fat can be harmful. Fat is a carrier for certain vitamins and essential fatty acids.

Young dogs need fat as much as older ones: just consider the relatively high fat content of canine milk. There are a number of fat sources.

Dog biscuits (with meat) are generally high in fat.

Vegetable oils (from sunflowers, soybeans, and corn) are a good source of essential fatty acids, and you should be sure to use them if you make up your own dog rations.

Rendered animal fat (lard, tallow, etc.) contains few essential fatty acids, but some believers say it is good for your beagle's coat; other people consider this nonsense.

Nearly lean meat is relatively useless as a source of essential fatty acids.

Vitamins

Vitamins are absolutely essential for the wellbeing of your beagle. There are a number of good sources.

Yeast in the form of baker's yeast or brewer's yeast, is a good addition to a dog's diet. It contains many vitamins, including the B complex and vitamins D and E. A knife-tip of yeast mixed into the feed stimulates the bacterial flora in the large intestine with positive results.

Cod-liver oil in its natural form is preferred over the synthetically constituted vitamins, principally because the synthetic products are too concentrated. Cod-liver oil has a high content of vitamins A, D, and E. A full-grown beagle with a body weight of approximately 20 pounds (9 kg) should get 1/3 teaspoon mixed into the feed daily. Buy natural cod-liver oil sold for human consumption; veterinary-grade cod-liver oil is generally not as refined.

Fruit is probably the best source of vitamins and minerals for your beagle. I particularly recommend juice from any of the tropical fruits and tomato juice. I'd provide it as a treat for your beagle, along with a regular serving of fruit in its diet. Many dogs have been trained to consider a piece of fruit as a reward for good performance, and if they have accomplished something special, they await their apple or orange with obvious joy.

The Proper Diet

Commercial Dog Food

Commercial dog food can save you a lot of time and trouble. You don't have to worry about balancing your beagle's rations. You also don't have to be concerned about contamination with germs of all kinds. Homemade feed is easily contaminated. Commercial preparations are made with strict quality control and can be trusted to remain germ free.

The high degree of competition in the preparation and sale of commercial dog food also provides the needed pressure to keep these products of high quality. They furnish good nutrition from good food sources in well-balanced proportions. The competition also keeps the price reasonable. Let me go into some detail to give you a better insight into the relative advantages of preparing your own dog rations or of using commercial feed.

Constant quality is guaranteed by a fully automated manufacturing process, guarded by research and quality control. All manufacturers are subject to federal (and, in some instances, state and local) regulations.

Quality control begins with the purchase of the raw ingredients and with the delivery of these ingredients to the factory. All manufacturers follow the standard of using only materials that are approved for human consumption. Complete dog food is manufactured with the federal standard *Nutrient Requirements of Domestic Animals* (National Academy of Science, Washington, D.C., 1974) in mind. The label (on box or can) generally gives a nutritional analysis of the contents and indicates the amounts to be fed to various breeds of dogs.

The quality of today's dog food is really quite high, and the manufacturers are correct in stating that people can safely make a meal of dog food.

Hygiene is maintained by making the ingredients germ free and keeping the manufacturing process pure. Manufacturers quickly and efficiently process such ingredients as meat and slaughter waste that are highly subject to spoilage, using the same methods and equipment as when packing meat for human consumption. This is especially true for frozen food and canned food. Canned dog food is always sterilized to kill germs, and the final product is heated to assure that there is no air in the can and that the can is properly sealed against re-entry of germs.

Mixed, compressed feed contains only ingredients that don't spoil easily. Again, the processing is performed at a high level of sanitation, and there really is no way you can surpass this in your own kitchen.

The shelf-life of commercial dog feed allows you to buy a good supply of food without worry about spoilage. You can put it in the pantry without need for precautions. The manufacturer takes this responsibility out of your hands.

By contrast, if you prepare your dog rations, you must constantly be on guard against spoilage. Meat and vegetables especially are highly perishable. You can preserve them by special processing, like cooking or freezing, but in practice this involves quite a bit of trouble. You just never know whether the meat you buy is contaminated despite the efforts of the meat-packing industry. A notable and dangerous contaminant is *Salmonella* bacteria.

The shelf-life of commercial food is always indicated on the labels of standard brands. Be sure that you take note of the pull date, so that you gain the full benefit of freshness. Buy only the amount of food in advance that can be used up before the expiration date.

Convenience is a key factor, given the busy lives most of us lead. The ready-made, well-balanced product can be trusted by conscientious owners to keep the feeding of their pets simple and fast. Large kennels naturally use commercial dog food. The time saved by the operators can be devoted to better care and training.

Dried dog food can be provided on a free-access basis, meaning that the beagle itself is allowed to determine the amount of food it consumes. A supply is made available day and night. In the beginning, a dog given free access to food is apt to overeat, but after a few days this will taper off. The dog acquires a sense of how much food it really needs. Free access to food is, naturally, easier on the owner; also, it can improve the pet's metabolism and temperament.

A young dog can learn to use a self-feeder at about four weeks of age. If you switch an older dog to self-feeding, do it all at once. Make sure that a self-feeding dog always has a supply of fresh, clean drinking water and enough exercise.

Acceptability is one of the potential problems with commercial dog food. Not all types are accepted by a particular dog. It is a question of individual differences in liking certain tastes and smells. Fortunately, there is more than enough variation in the types of dog food that are available. There are compressed and expanded dry feeds, dog dinners for warm meals, canned food, soft-moist or semimoist food, and the like. There are many brands of each, so you ought to be able to find one brand and preparation that your beagle will accept.

Types of Dog Food

In view of the wide variety of products on the commercial market, it is worthwhile to give this subject closer attention.

Dried feed can generally be provided without further preparation. It comes in dehydrated pieces, pellets, and balls that contain no more than 10–12% moisture. If you use it, your beagle will drink more than if you feed moist food, but that doesn't mean that it should drink excessively. If excessive water intake does occur, switch to another kind of feed. If your beagle still drinks too much, consult your veterinarian.

Most commercial dried feed provides complete nutrition and furnishes all the required food elements. Many ingredients are ground and mixed together to achieve this desired balance. Some are of plant origin, because this is an inexpensive way to provide protein. A prime example of this are soy pellets, which undergo a special manufacturing process. Many manufacturers of dried feed also use meat wastes, which provide a higher quality of protein but cost more money. The same is true of meat or fish meal. As long as the overall analysis for protein satisfies the dog's nutritional

requirements, the source material isn't very important.

Many commercial dried dog feeds are rather low in fat. The manufacturers want to avoid a soft product that falls apart during transportation and is crumbly by the time you buy it. Furthermore, a higher fat content can cause feed to become rancid and more subject to spoilage. Some manufacturers take care of the fat deficiency by spraying the food with a layer of fat at the end of the manufacturing process. If the brand you use isn't treated that way, I recommend you supplement the feed, especially during the winter. Simply add a few drops of oil (corn, sunflower, or soybean, for example) when you fill you beagle's bowl.

You can soak dried food in water if you like (and if your beagle likes it!).

Some brands of dried dog feed contain food coloring and taste enhancers to increase the appeal of the product for human and dog. Some people worry about whether this is right, but at least you can rest assured that dog food manufacturers use only those additives that are approved for human consumption.

Let's look in more detail at the various forms in which you can buy dried dog food.

Dog biscuits are baked into the familiar bone-shaped or square pieces. The type that contains meat generally has cracklings in it, which are poorly tolerated by many dogs and can cause severe diarrhea. The meatless biscuit can be combined with fresh or canned meat, separately or mixed together. Check the label to see whether the biscuit you're buying is intended as a complete food or should be supplemented. Dog biscuits and bits make a good snack for your beagle and can be given as a reward for good behavior.

Extruded or compressed dried feed is manufactured by grinding and mixing the constituents and then putting them, in the form of a mash, through a sieve under pressure. The diameter of the holes in the sieve determines the eventual size of the pieces, which are made in different sizes for young and adult dogs. Puppy-sized pieces also have different ingredients to fulfill the special needs of the young animal. Feeding the small,

The Proper Diet

grainy pieces to puppies can result in quite a bit of waste, but this can be minimized by buying the right kind of puppy feeding dish.

Compressed dried feed is generally grayish in color, caused in part by the binder. In many cases molasses is used for this purpose.

Expanded dried feed is manufactured by grinding and mixing the constituents and then forcing the mash under pressure through a tube with a gradually tapering diameter. When the mash reaches the small end of the tube, the pressure is suddenly released, causing the product to swell. This results in pieces that are porous and much harder than the compressed product.

This process has the advantage of promoting digestibility, brought about by the unlocking of the nutrients. It also mixes the ingredients better, and because the product is hard, it promotes mechanical cleaning of your beagle's teeth.

Dog dinners are another variant of the complete, dried feed. Some of the ingredients remain in their normal, unground form, including expanded corn, rolled wheat, and pieces of dried vegetables. The other ingredients are added in the form of little pieces.

These dinners fill the demand of dog owners who want to give their pets a warm meal of the type they themselves enjoy. The dinner is prepared by pouring warm water or warm milk over it and letting it soak.

The moist dinner doesn't provide natural cleaning for your beagle's teeth; in fact, the food tends to stick between the teeth. You can counteract this by giving your beagle a rawhide or nylon bone and brushing its teeth regularly (see page 24).

Soft-moist feed and **semimoist feed** are complete rations with high digestibility. The biologic rating of soft-moist feed is generally somewhat higher than that of meat, and it is excellent for your beagle. The moisture content of soft-moist feed lies between that of dried feed and canned feed, about 25%. Almost all dogs like it, probably because it more closely resembles meat. It is a general rule that dogs like a food to the extent it resembles meat—and the moister, the better!

Offal and waste meat from packing houses form the basis for this dog feed. The meat is quickly cleaned and processed. The processing is rather expensive, adding to the retail cost of the product, but you may well feel that your beagle is worth the price. The soft feed is quite suitable for puppies and for sick or old dogs. Again, remember that if you feed soft feed, you have to pay more attention to the care of your beagle's teeth.

Canned food retains about 75% of the natural moisture in meat and vegetables. The well-known brands contain meat that was subjected to scientific quality control and broken into small pieces. Weighed quantitites of meat are mixed with about 20 other constituents. This variety promotes a high nutritional value.

The mix is put into cans by machines, the cans are sealed, and then the whole is carefully sterilized so that it will keep. The cans are checked to be sure no air remained inside and that the seal is thorough.

The process of preparing canned food includes careful attention to providing ingredients in the proper proportions. The process is excellent for preserving vitamin B, which is 80% destroyed if food is cooked in an open pot. The result is a true, complete food of excellent quality that dogs eat with gusto.

Canned food is also expensive, compared with dried feed, but if your beagle likes it, why not let it enjoy its meal? Supplement canned food with hard biscuits, which help scour the dog's teeth.

An important note: Don't supplement complete feeds with extra vitamins and minerals. The manufacturer has carefully put in the right

Any beagle should be exercised every day. An obese dog (top) loses its natural resistance, and its life span is likely to be short. This dog's diet should be lighter in fat and heavier in raw fiber.

Bottom: A properly proportioned beagle is notoriously healthy and robust. Typically, it will have "the wear-and-tear look of the hound that can last in the chase and follow its quarry to the death" (*The American Standard*).

34

amounts of these items, and providing more can be dangerous for your beagle. You can check the analysis on the label to assure yourself that vitamins and minerals have been added. Too high a level of certain vitamins can be poisonous, and added minerals can destroy the carefully calibrated calcium-phosphorus ratio in the feed.

Feeding Puppies

Before birth, the developing puppy is fed via the umbilical cord. The mother beagle provides it with all the nourishment needed for its growth. This all changes at whelping. The umbilical cord is severed, and the puppy has to feed itself. Once mother beagle has licked it dry, it gropes its way to the new source of nourishment. When it has reached the environs of the teats, the puppy makes upward motions with its head until it has found a nipple.

A healthy puppy naturally takes the nipple in its mouth and enjoys long drafts of warm milk. Its front legs make small kicks against the teats, which, along with the sucking, releases a hormone that stimulates milk production. The puppy's actions also stimulate contraction of the uterus, which promotes the speedy delivery of any puppies that still are in the womb.

During the first few days of lactation, the mother dog produces colostrum, which is high in protein and rich in antibodies. The antibodies protect the little ones from infectious diseases against which the mother has been vaccinated, or from which she has recovered. It is quite important for puppies to receive this colostrum.

Beagles, like other scent hounds, are known to roam and often get lost. Therefore, your dog should wear a collar with its registration number and a name tag—especially if it is a city dog! A tattoo on the inside of one ear can also help prove its identity.

How long maternal antibodies protect puppies can be determined by serological analysis. It depends principally on the quantity of antibodies available in the female's blood. Generally, you can assume that puppies are protected until about the seventh week of age. In any event, I suggest you check with your veterinarian as soon as possible to arrange for vaccination.

Dog's milk is rich in fat, which puppies need to develop subcutaneous connective tissue. Puppies don't make much use of the calcium and phosphorus in the milk until they are almost 6 weeks old, the stage at which the calcification of the bones first gets solidly underway.

Make sure that the mother dog lactates properly. If not, you will have to step in and help (see page 45). You can tell whether each puppy is developing properly by weighing the litter every day. If one of the puppies falls behind in weight, supplement the mother's milk with bottle feeding.

I strongly suggest that you prepare fully for bottle feeding well before you expect a new litter. Naturally, the first thing you need is a bottle. For beagle puppies, an ordinary baby bottle is fine. Be sure that the opening in the nipple isn't too large or too small and that the milk flows through it readily.

Artificial milk formula can be bought commercially, in powder form or completely ready to feed. The powder can be kept fresh longer, but you have to mix it with water. Be sure to follow the manufacturer's directions carefully. Check the completed mix for clumps by using a fine-mesh sieve; you can rub the clumps through the sieve with a spoon and then pour the mix through the sieve again until the clumps are properly dissolved. Never discard the clumps, because this alters the composition of the milk.

You also need a good thermometer to be sure that you provide the milk at the right temperature: 98.4°–102.2°F, (37°–39°C).

If your puppy won't take an artificial nipple, start it off with a few drops of milk sprinkled on the tongue.

If a puppy stops drinking from the bottle it may well be that it has had enough, or it may just be fooling around. You can tell the difference by pulling the nipple partway out of its mouth. If it is still hungry, it will start sucking again. Also, be guided by the directions furnished by the manufacturer on how much and how often puppies should be fed.

Supplementary Feeding

About three to four weeks after birth, you must supplement the feed of all puppies. A great many beagle breeders start with a combination of cooked cereal and ground meat. You can make up the hot cereal from a combination of old brown bread, oats, and the like, in milk. The most commonly used meat is ground beef, raw beef, or head cheese with nothing added.

If you want to get the puppies used to eating by themselves as soon as possible, it's best to keep the hot-cereal phase as short as possible. Switch to a commercial feed, soaked in milk if desired. Most commercial puppy feed is of good quality.

I recommend against trying to make up your own puppy feed. Many beginners in the beagle puppy-breeding business tend to underrate the importance of a properly balanced meal. Puppies have to grow at the proper rate, and to achieve the correct composition of the feed takes time and experience.

Dry feeds for puppies often come as grains and should be soaked before being fed. Soft-moist feed is softer and moister than dry feed, as the name indicates. It can cause problems by becoming sticky and adhering to the palate if it is chewed too long. If you are on the lookout for this problem, however, you can take the proper countermeasures.

Canned feed, especially the complete canned feeds put out by brand name manufacturers, can make good puppy feed because of its high moisture content, but you have to make sure that the pieces of meat aren't too large.

When you start supplementing the feed of your puppies, also be sure to provide water. Use a shallow puppy sized bowl so that there's no chance of the puppy's drowning in it.

Depending on the size of the litter, furnish food three to six times per day.

Some females are in the habit of regurgitating food for their puppies at this stage of their development. This looks awful but is quite normal for dogs. They act just like wild canids that regurgitate partially digested feed for their young. Puppies seem to like eating it, and they often stimulate their mother to regurgitate by licking her around the snout.

Once puppies are around six weeks old, the mother beagle will have stopped lactating almost completely and will pay less attention to her litter. Typically, the mother will have kept the whelping box quite clean, but this cleanliness diminishes at the time of supplementary feeding. This means more work for the breeder.

Feeding Growing Dogs

Typically, young beagles get a new home some time after weaning. If you are the new owner, be sure to ask the breeder how he or she has been

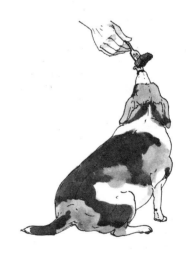

If you offer your beagle tidbits from the table, you should not be surprised if it ends up being overweight.

feeding the puppies. It is important that the dog receive the same food in the beginning as it did in its "old home." If you want to switch to another type of feed, do it very gradually (over a period of 4 to 5 days) and with appropriate care.

Stick to a complete feed, don't overfeed, and don't supplement with vitamins and minerals unless your veterinarian recommends this. Not infrequently, dogs are overindulged and oversupplemented. When this causes nutritional deficiencies, people often ask for "an extra shot of vitamins," surely the worst thing to do at that time. To avoid problems, don't let beagles (or any dog, for that matter) get fat.

Gradually, the young beagle can get the same feed as the grown dog, although in different quantities. I recommend weighing the animal from time to time and checking the weight against the recommended weight for its age according to the standard table you can get from your veterinarian.

When putting out feed and water for your beagle, be sure that you place the bowls at chest height. This keeps the dog from crouching while eating or drinking.

Feeding the Grown Dog

You can use a complete dog food year after year without problems, if it is a good-quality brand. Be guided by the beagle's preferences, which you will have discovered by now. Our modern world moves fast, so you may find that your favorite dog food is replaced by another product. I wouldn't worry much about this, because it is likely to be an improved product, given the competition in the marketplace. Beagle and owner both benefit if the manufacturer makes the best product at the lowest price.

Instead of a commercial food, you can also make up your own if you like (see pages 29–31). The important thing is that your beagle grows up normally. If you notice any deviations or problems, be sure to get professional advice, generally from your veterinarian. Don't skimp on getting

advice even though it costs you money. In the long run, it costs even more to consult with someone who supposedly knows "something" about dog care but then gives you the wrong advice.

A note on exercise for your beagle puppy: Don't force it to overdo things. In most cases, the young dog itself will give you hints on how much and how fast it wants to exercise. Get the dog used to exercising gradually. Don't rush the dog into running along with you if you bicycle for exercise. Work up to this gradually when your beagle reaches approximately a year of age.

Feeding Pregnant and Lactating Dams

The moment you plan to breed your female beagle, make sure she is in top condition. Remember, puppies need to draw the best nourishment possible from their mothers while they are in the womb.

During the first three weeks, the puppies don't grow much, but during the second half of the pregnancy, they grow rapidly and take in about twice as much foodstuff as during the first half. Consult your veterinarian about the precise food requirements of the pregnant female beagle.

Remember that quality is even more important than quantity in considering the feeding of a pregnant bitch (female). The biologic value of the protein is of particular importance. Don't skimp on quality!

After whelping, the puppies must be nourished by dog milk, which again draws on the body of the mother, (dam). Be sure to keep up quality nutrition for the lactating dam. Immediately after whelping, again consult your veterinarian. The *Nutrient Requirements of Domestic Animals* (see pg. 32) is a good reference for precise detail on proper diet.

During both pregnancy and lactation, be sure your female beagle doesn't run into deficiencies in calcium, phosphorus, or the vitamin B complex. This will prevent her from getting a number of deficiency-related diseases.

Raising Beagles

It's best not to let a female breed before she is two years of age or when she has been in heat at least twice. If you breed her earlier, there is a good chance that she has not attained full growth herself. More specifically, when a bitch first comes into heat her pelvic bones are set and she will not get any taller. She will, however, mature in muscle mass and tone, which are the important considerations.

Estrus, and What to Do About It

Most beagle females first come into heat (estrus) when they are about nine months of age. Generally, they come back into heat every six months. You notice the onset of heat by the swelling of the vulva, the only externally visible female reproductive organs. Many females start to emit odors during this premenstrual period. Attracted by the odor, males approach the female, sniff under her tail, and at times a male makes an attempt to mount. Generally, the female doesn't appreciate this attempt and growls at the male. At the start of true heat, the vulva swells to the maximum extent, and a bloody exudate is noticeable. This exudate is quite different from the menstrual bleeding of women. Human menstruation occurs during the degenerative phase of the changes in the wall of the womb, but the exudate of bitches flows during the generative phase. The bloody exudate continues about 10 days. Internally, two important changes are occurring. First, several ova ripen in the ovaries, and second, the wall of the womb thickens so that it is ready to receive the resulting embryos if the ova are fertilized.

After 10 days, the exudate becomes lighter in color, and several days later it can be completely clear. In this period, breeding can take place.

After 14 – 15 days the exudate practically stops. After that, the swelling of the vulva decreases, and three weeks after the onset of true heat everything appears to have returned to normal.

If your female beagle follows this typical pattern, she can be bred on the tenth through twelfth days.

Unfortunately, many females don't stick to this schedule. Some of them allow mounting on the third day of heat. Others won't permit mounting until the twentieth day. In most cases, the tenth day is best for a successful mating, but there is an enormous range of favorable days for breeding. You yourself must determine the right days for your own female dogs.

The Stud

Males that have had several satisfactory matings can be considered acceptable studs and should be able to maintain the characteristics of the breed properly. If they hadn't done well in earlier matings, people would have stopped using them for breeding purposes.

All males that have been exhibited at dog shows were examined by the judges who determined that they had two normal testicles. Participation is no guarantee of quality, however, since any AKC-registered dog may enter. It's best, of course, to arrange for a breeding female to be covered by a male that has received high marks at a show.

The penis of the male dog has a somewhat unusual build. A small bone inside it keeps the penis fairly stiff even in periods without sexual stimulation. Also, the penis contains two areas that can expand considerably, especially the posterior of the two. During mating, this highly swollen segment is usually completely inserted into the vagina. The female can contract the muscles of the vagina quite strongly, preventing the male from retracting the penis (the so-called "tie"). The two are thoroughly locked, a situation that can persist for some time, ranging from several to 45 minutes. When the female calms down and relaxes, her vaginal muscles also relax, and the engorged penis becomes more flaccid as the blood drains away. Then the penis can be withdrawn.

Raising Beagles

Mating

When a female is ready for intercourse, she stands still before a male and raises her tail and bends it sideways. This totally bares her vulva. The male rears up on his hind legs and clasps his forelegs around the belly of the female. Next, the male tries to direct his penis toward the vulva, an effort that the dog owner can assist.

To be sure that the female is properly impregnated, many breeders let her mate again two days later—naturally with the same male. The thought behind this practice is to ensure that viable sperm are present at the same time the ripe ova enter the oviduct.

Since egg cells mature gradually, however, you don't want to take a chance and let a female roam while she is in heat, even if she has already been mated. Some females are quite ready to let themselves be mounted again by a strange male. You find out about this when she gives birth: There may be different types of puppies in the litter!

Pregnancy

After mating, you have a nine week's wait. At first, there is no visible indication to assure yourself that a bitch is indeed pregnant. Gradually, however, the bitch gains weight and slows her activities. You may be able to notice movement of pups in the womb as early as the fifth week.

As stated, an average pregnancy lasts 63 days, but some deviation is possible. So that you have a better idea of when whelping will start, I suggest taking your dog's temperature three times per day, starting on day 55. You can use an ordinary rectal thermometer (see page 52). Normal canine temperature is about 101.5° F (38.5° C). About 24 hours before whelping begins, you will see a sharp drop to below 98.6° F (37° C). As soon as you notice the temperature dropping, take a new reading every hour. After several hours, the reading will go up again. You can expect whelping to begin 24 hours after the low point in your temperature readings.

False Pregnancy

Females can fool you with a false pregnancy. For nine weeks, they can faithfully show all symptoms of pregnancy. At the end of this period, they even begin to prepare a nest and milk can flow from their nipples. But no pups appear.

This phenomenon is caused by a minor hormonal derangement that happens to persist about as long as a pregnancy. However, if you know your female hasn't been mated, you can suspect false pregnancy. Some bitches show signs of false pregnancy after every heat period. On the other hand, if you have arranged a mating, false pregnancy can lead to real disappointment. To clear any doubt, have your veterinarian examine your dog.

Preparations

Most pregnancies run their course without difficulty. Sometimes the hormonal shifts cause a female to have an increased appetite the first few weeks, but don't give in to it. The first couple of weeks, the embryos hardly grow at all, and if you overfeed the mother, she gets fatter and more lethargic, which can cause problems at whelping.

During the second half of pregnancy and certainly the last three weeks, the female's appetite increases appropriately because at that time the fetuses grow enormously fast. In some cases, a bitch has to be fed two or even three times the normal ration.

About the sixth or seventh week of pregnancy, start getting the female accustomed to the whelping box and whelping room.

Signs that the pregnancy is coming to an end include nesting behavior. Often the female keeps rearranging the bedding in the whelping box. For example, she may scratch and tear the newspapers you put down. You will also be able to see her nipples swell. As stated, you should take her temperature two to three times per day after the 55th day. Also be sure to alert your veterinarian at least two weeks before you expect the puppies.

In selecting a whelping room, give thought to finding a quiet place. I would avoid such locations as a corner of the kitchen or den. I would also advise against using the garage or shed. Those places are too cold and drafty and too far away for you to be able to keep an eye on the litter. You might miss an early sign that something is going wrong.

Generally, I would choose a bedroom. From the viewpoint of the litter, the best bedroom is your own. With the whelping box placed there, you'll be able to keep a close watch over the litter without leaving your bed, but be prepared to cope with a lot of new, strange sounds. If you don't want your rest disturbed like that for a couple of weeks, you might want to select another bedroom. Many breeders do so.

The equipment you'll want to get ready before whelping starts includes a sterilized, somewhat blunt pair of scissors, a navel bandage, a disinfectant, cotton balls, towels, and a scale. Many breeders don't bother with a scale, but I think it's important to monitor the body weight of puppies. At birth, beagles weigh between 8.8 and 12.3 ounces (250 and 350 g), and eight to ten days later, this weight should have doubled. You should weigh your pups daily and note their progress.

The Whelping Box

Dogs naturally nest in hollows, and they love a quiet, comfortable nesting place. It should be snug but not inaccessible for you. I suggest a whelping box about as long as it is wide and big enough to allow your beagle female to be stretched out along the sides. Measure her from the tip of the nose to the base of the tail. Don't worry about the tail itself.

Many breeders make a special effort to keep a bitch from lying on her pups because her relatively heavy weight could kill a little one. These people build a rail along the side of the box under which the pups can lie without danger. I don't consider this precaution essential for a mother dog with healthy reflexes, but the rail certainly can't do any harm.

The sides of the box should be high enough so the beagle can stand up straight. Maintain at least this height if you want to put a cover on the whelping box. A lid isn't essential, however, and you definitely should not use one if you want to warm the box with a heat lamp. High walls are good. They prevent drafts, which are even worse for puppies than cold temperatures per se.

Cut the top down on one of the sides, so the female can get in and out of the box easily, or provide a removable side. When the pups are just whelped, you can put a single slat across the opening to keep them in. Add a second slat when the pups become older and more exploratory. Still later, add a third slat.

A good heat source is important. Some people use an infrared lamp or a pig lamp, but I don't recommend this type of heater. It radiates heat from only one direction, so that pups that don't move around much may get too hot on one side and too cold on the other side of their bodies. This can cause real problems in itself. Also, these ray lamps create dry air, which really is bad for the pups.

Contact heat is better, and you can provide it with a large heating pad. These electrically heated pads are at least 39½ x 23½ inches (100 x 60 cm). Some brands have a thermostat to adjust the heat; others are not adjustable. Install the pad under the whelping box so that about half the floor space is heated. In winter, I recommend placing the whelping box within a few feet of the radiator of the whelping room.

Keep the temperature of the floor of the box at about 75.2° F (24° C) for the first 10–14 days after whelping. After that, you can reduce the temperature gradually until it reaches room temperature at the end of the third week.

The best bedding for the whelping box is newspaper. The ink can rub off on the dog, but that doesn't really matter. Newspaper is extremely cheap and quite absorbent. During the birth process, a lot of amniotic fluid is released, so that highly absorbent bedding is particularly important.

You can improve the bedding after whelping by

placing a sheet or blanket over the paper. Be sure to change the cover frequently, as well as the bedding. Wash the cover in hot water.

Birth

Just before whelping, most beagle mothers are quite nervous, especially if they haven't had young before. They pace nervously, scratch at the bedding until the newspapers are shredded, and jump up and then drop down heavily. They pant hard. No one can help notice that something is going to happen.

Birth itself begins with contractions. At first, only the wall of the womb contracts, but after some time the cramps are worsened through pressure from the diaphragm. The female dog groans when the diaphragm puts strong pressure on the womb. The combined pressure moves the pups in the direction of the vagina, which now functions as a birth canal.

The birth of the first puppy is usually announced by rupture of the amniotic sac, which liberates a good quantity of liquid. No matter how hard the female has to work to deliver her pups, she still finds time to frequently lick her vulva and lap up the amniotic fluid.

Generally, pups are born with the front feet first followed by the head, but don't get upset if the hind legs come out first. Generally, a reverse birth causes no problems in dogs. With one or two strong contractions, the puppy is pushed entirely free.

Many bitches lie down during whelping, and the newborn puppy is shoved along the floor. Others give birth standing up, so that the puppies fall a certain distance to the floor. The fall seems scary to the on-looker, but almost every puppy survives it. So, don't worry.

Aftercare

Puppies can come into the world undraped, but often they are wrapped in part of the amniotic sac.

Be sure to take off those pieces, especially from the puppy's head. You want to be sure nothing interferes with proper breathing. The mother dog usually takes care of this, but sometimes a bitch is so nervous that she tends to neglect her newborn. When she gives signs that she doesn't have a good sense of what is going on, you have to jump in to help.

Next, the umbilical cord has to be severed. Most puppies are born together with the placenta, or afterbirth, which is eaten by the mother dog. As she does so, she chews through the umbilical cord, but keep an eye on the procedure. As a last resort, if the mother doesn't sever the cord, you must do it for her. Use the blunt scissors you prepared for the purpose, and cut the cord about 7/8–1 1/4 inches (2–3 cm) from the pup's belly. Blunt scissors squeeze the blood vessels as you cut, so that very little blood is spilled.

See to it that the mother (dam) doesn't bite off the cord too closely to the body. Some mothers keep chewing away until they create a hole in the body of the pup. If there is a cut in the navel or a small tear in the tummy, a veterinarian can sew up the problem. Be sure to prevent this if possible, though, and certainly avoid deep wounds.

As soon as a puppy gets up, it must be dried off. Most beagle dams lick off their young diligently and often rather roughly. This makes the puppies cry, but it doesn't matter much. Actually, the cries provide assurance that the puppy is alive and well.

If the dam neglects her puppies, dry them yourself with a towel. Feel free to rub. Just stroking the puppy with the towel doesn't dry it properly.

Also pay attention to the mouth, especially if a puppy has had a difficult birth. If the process took a long time, it may have swalllowed some amniotic fluid. That's not bad if it is swallowed properly. If some leaked into the lungs, however, the puppy may be uncomfortable. You will know this is a potential problem if you see a lot of liquid and slime in the little mouth. This must be removed, and forcefully so. Rub the puppy dry; then take solid hold of it so that it can't squirm, and swing it several times, head down. The motion of the swing and the force of gravity will remove most of the slime and liquid from the mouth.

As soon as the puppy is dry and breathes quietly, lay it alongside the mother beagle. Some newborn pups seem extremely hungry and immediately look for a nipple. The sucking stimulates the mother beagle hormonally to give birth to the following puppies. So you can let the puppy suck without worry, but do stay in the neighborhood.

At the following birth, a mother may start pacing and turning, and the first-born pup may get in the way. Although a newborn puppy seems to be able to take a lot of abuse, it can be killed if it has to bear the brunt of its mother's full weight. That's why many breeders remove pups as they are born and lay them together in a nice, warm cozy corner until the entire litter has been delivered.

Successive puppies are born just like the first one. First you see the amniotic fluid, then the puppy. The new pup has to be dried and swung around if slime has to be removed from its little mouth. Meanwhile, the mother beagle eats the afterbirth which contains hormones that can favorably affect the birth process. Keep in mind that each portion of afterbirth is a meal in itself. After the fourth or fifth portion, the mother may lose the strength needed for expelling the last-born puppies. For that reason, many breeders remove the remaining afterbirth.

Sometimes, a dam wants to take a break after the birth of a puppy and the processing that goes with it. It's all right to let the beagle out to exercise, urinate, and defecate. Encourage her to relieve herself, because a full bladder or intestine interferes with proper whelping. You want to provide all the internal room possible to let the puppies pass easily.

During such a break, you can also give the dam something to drink. Many breeders provide just water, but if she likes it, you can also give her coffee with some milk and sugar. This will give her a bit of extra pep!

Successive births follow one another at changing intervals. A couple of puppies can be born very closely together, but generally the interval lasts a half-hour or longer. If the interval extends to more than two or three hours, the veterinarian can give the mother an injection to stimulate the contractions. Or, he or she may conclude the mother needs a cesarean. Another outcome may be that the veterinarian concludes tentatively that all the pups have been whelped. I call this a "tentative" conclusion because the veterinarian can't feel puppies that may be left far back inside the pelvis and may also have a problem feeling those that lie far toward the front, inside the rib cage.

The entire whelping process may seem to take an eternity, but after several hours of real time, things quiet down. Let the mother beagle out for some exercise, and meanwhile take the little ones out of the box and clean it for them. When the mother beagle returns, put the puppies at her nipples and let them suck and rest.

The Checkup

When you have caught your breath, think of items of care you may have overlooked. Did you weigh the puppies at birth? If not, do it now.

Check each puppy carefully. They are born with closed eyes, which after 10–11 days open slowly.

The nose should be sound. A small split in the nose may point to a split palate, which may occur even if there isn't a true harelip. Look inside the mouth to make sure. Don't keep puppies with a harelip. They have real trouble sucking and starve if you don't have them euthanized.

Next, check the abdomen. With a little practice, you'll be able to sex the puppies. Young males don't show testicles, but the penis lies considerably more forward than does the vulva of the females. Be sure not to confuse the navel stem for a penis.

Finally, check the tail and anus. The first day of life, you will see the *meconium* coming out of the anus. This refers to the waste products that accumulated in the intestines during the fetal period. It must be eliminated before the puppy gets a good appetite to start sucking.

Raising Beagles

If you notice anything wrong, consult your veterinarian immediately. He or she can give you the advice you need to be sure the pups grow into healthy and alert dogs!

Cesarean Operations

If your veterinarian had to help assure safe whelping by doing a cesarean, you'll have extra work with aftercare. The dam will still be dazed from the anesthesia, while the puppies are active and hungry. You will have to help feed and care for them for one or two days. Lay them at the nipples, and after they have sucked, massage their bellies and around the anus. Use moist cotton balls for this job. They need the massage to relieve themselves properly. If you don't massage them, they become constipated, which can be a fatal problem in young pups.

Nursing

Colostrum
Colostrum is the first milk produced by the dam. It contains antibodies against all the diseases for which the mother was innoculated or from which she has recovered. During their first 48 hours of life, the puppies take in these antibodies, which then protect them against these diseases.

If the mother doesn't lactate during the first 48 hours, the puppies miss important protection. You will have to make up for this as much as possible. Maintain excellent hygiene, and don't allow your puppies near strange dogs. Consult with your veterinarian so you can have the puppies vaccinated at the earliest effective time.

Poor Lactation
You have to hand-raise the puppies if the mother lactates poorly or not at all, or in the sad case that she dies during whelping.

You can put together a simple drink to tide over puppies while their mother is recovering from a cesarean. Boil some water, let it cool, and then add glucose and a pinch of salt. Or you can mix about 7 ounces (200 ml) of sterilized milk with two egg yolks.

For a complete milk substitute, use commercially prepared milk powder. Some brands are about as good as real dog's milk. You need only add boiled and cooled water. Feed the puppies by letting them suck from bottles, which are available commercially.

Puppies need to drink frequently, especially at first. Expect to feed them every two to three hours. After 7–10 days, you can cut down the frequency provided the puppies are growing and gaining properly. Strong puppies can be fed every five to six hours. You'll know they're doing all right if they don't whimper hungrily but snooze and snore quietly in the box.

Remember to keep massaging the bellies with moist cotton balls after every meal. Make broad strokes across the belly from the ribs to the pelvis. If they start to urinate and defecate, you'll know you have done it right. Don't worry, however, if there is no defecation after each meal. Sometimes the puppies urinate only.

A mother beagle with pups that are ready to be weaned.

45

Raising Beagles

Caring for the Puppies

Weak Puppies

Sometimes a litter seems to pine away within a week after whelping. The puppies don't gain, but lose weight. After a week to 10 days they are so weak that they start dying. Even a veterinarian may not know what to do.

A possible problem may be incompatible blood types. If the dam is A negative and some or all of the puppies are A positive, she builds up antibodies to the puppies' blood. After whelping, these antibodies appear in the colostrum. Puppies drinking the antibodies do poorly because the antibodies break down their red blood corpuscles.

Other causes are harder to pin down. If the puppies have a virus infection, then often something can be done for them. Other than providing environmental support, however, you can't do much for many weak pups.

Environmental support consists of temperature control. First, raise the ambient temperature in the whelping box to about 87° F (30° C). After 3 weeks, lower it gradually to 68° F (20° C). Heat helps kill off viruses.

More common is the situation in which a mother decides to do away with a runt. You'll see the little one lie at the dam's backside instead of at the nipples. Apparently, the runt is neglected because of its low body temperature. The usual temperature of puppies is normally one to two degrees lower than that of the mother beagle. If a puppy is cold or is poorly nourished, its temperature can drop to below 87° F (30° C).

If you want to improve a puppy's chances of living, you need to warm its body slowly. It won't do to put it under a heat lamp. That causes the puppy to dry out. It's better to warm it by holding it against your own body.

Next, see to it that the puppy has energy for producing its own body heat. It won't work to have the mother beagle nurse it. I also advise against giving milk substitute to the puppy. The puppy won't be able to digest it because its stomach temperature is even lower than its basic body temperature. If you get milk into the stomach, the milk curdles.

You need to make up a special sugar solution. Put glucose and a pinch of salt into water that was boiled and then cooled. Keep the temperature of the solution at least at body temperature—about 98.6° F (37° C). Drip some of the solution into the puppy's mouth, at first every 15 minutes, then every 30 minutes, and finally every hour. By the way, the reason for putting a little salt into the solution is to help prevent dehydration.

The whole process of warming the puppy and feeding it by hand can take many hours. You need to stay with the little one until it shows activity and can raise its head. Then you can put it back into the box with its mother. If she then accepts it, you have saved its little life!

When the Eyes Open

During their first 10 days of life, puppies are completely helpless. They feel their way through the whelping box and generally know to find their source of milk. If they stray too far from the mother beagle, she can take the puppies in her mouth and bring them back where they ought to be.

About the tenth or eleventh day, the eyes slowly open. The process can take a few days; one eye can be ahead of the other or open in a different way.

The opening of its eyes ushers in a new stage of life for a puppy. It has to absorb many more impressions than it did the first 10 days. The puppy becomes more curious and starts crawling farther away from the mother beagle. However, don't change the daily care and feeding until about the twentieth day.

Worming and Supplementary Feeding

Puppies are frequently born with an infestation of intestinal roundworms, and about the third week of life, you need to expect that they have adult roundworms in their intestines. At that time, they need their first worming.

Raising Beagles

Any larvae that are still present in the intestines aren't removed by the anthelmintic. So worming must be done weekly for three weeks to be sure that most, if not all of the worms have developed to a stage where they can be killed.

Heavily infested dogs get a "wormy stomach," an enormous swelling of the stomach. This comes about because roundworms rob the puppy's body of protein. Protein, among other functions, helps distribute moisture in the body. Protein deficiency causes an accumulation of moisture in places where there shouldn't be any. Puppies swell mainly in the stomach.

You should get ready to start supplementary feeding one or two days after the first worming. In fact, you should start sooner if the female doesn't produce enough milk to feed her pups. Part of the supplement can be baby cereal, which you should prepare with dog milk substitute.

About the same time, you can get the puppies used to solid food. Many breeders offer a small portion of cooked hamburger meat, starting the third week. You can also use finely sliced canned meat or soft-moist feed. Dry feed can't be handled by puppies at that age, not even if it is soaked in milk or water.

Weaning

Expect lactation of the female to decrease between the third and sixth weeks after whelping. Increase supplementary feeding accordingly. About the sixth week, puppies should be ready for weaning, so during the previous three weeks you will have to gradually increase the amount of meat, soft-moist feed, or canned food, along with a serving of cereal from time to time. Provide water for drinking.

The amount of food needed by puppies of that age is considerable, but the size of their stomachs is relatively small. I strongly suggest you provide four to six meals per day, even though it is more work than feeding once or twice daily.

Around the sixth week, you can separate the puppies from their mother. Many breeders give the puppies a great degree of freedom at this point and let the mother dog join her puppies only when she herself feels like it. When the puppies get the chance, they will rush toward their mother in order to try to suckle again. Most mothers won't have any milk to give or very little, but that doesn't keep the little ones from trying.

At this stage, the pups have developed teeth, and sucking can hurt their mother's nipples considerably, so mother beagle will not enjoy being with her pups for very long. You can remove her from their quarters to give her relief. You can build some kind of platform to which the mother can jump. Puppies of that age can run well, but they can't jump much at all. From her perch, the mother beagle can watch them without being stormed!

Leave-taking

You can have the new owners pick up their puppies when they are eight to nine weeks old. Saying goodbye to the little ones can tug at your heartstrings. After all, you just spent eight to nine weeks raising the pups from newborns to young dogs, and with all the effort you put into the task, you surely will have become attached to them. Good sense tells you that you must let them go nonetheless.

Don't consider the goodbye to be forever. If you wish, arrange to visit your former puppies from time to time. The new owners will understand your continued interest in the puppies' welfare even though they are no longer in your care.

If Your Beagle Gets Sick

The ultimate responsibility for your beagle's health is yours, but clearly you can't take care of everything yourself. Your most important adviser is your veterinarian. You have a broad choice of veterinarians, but once you select one, I suggest you stick with him or her as long as you don't have a well-founded reason for changing. Don't run from one veterinarian to another. Don't go to one for worming your beagle and to another for vaccinations, and so on. The veterinarian needs to know the medical history of your beagle and needs to have a certain relationship with you, the owner.

All veterinarians are taught the same basic information about dog health, but you can't expect your veterinarian to be equally skilled in every area. Good veterinarians will refer you to specialists if they come up against problems they can't handle, or they may refer you to the clinic at the university.

In addition to therapeutic help, your veterinarian should also be a source of general information. Some give too little advice. They may not have the

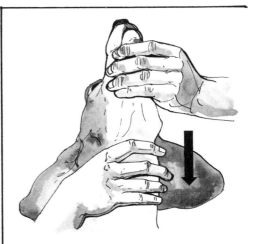

Rub the throat to make sure that the dog actually swallows its medication.

time, or they may not be convinced that a concerned owner wants to know what is wrong with a dog and the prospects of treatment. Don't, however, hesitate to ask. You have the right to information about your beagle, and if reasonable inquiries are ignored, look elsewhere. I don't think this will happen too often.

Be reasonable in dealing with your veterinarian. The fact that you pay for services doesn't give you the right to telephone at impossible hours for a consultation—certainly not if your dog has been sick for some time.

Your veterinarian should be able to expect certain things from you. You ought to have basic knowledge about the health care of your beagle, including worming, parasite control, vaccination, and nutrition. If you study this book, you will have this basic knowledge.

If your beagle does get sick, be sure to follow the instructions of your veterinarian carefully. You don't want to give the impression that no matter what is suggested, the treatment will not go anywhere because of your lack of involvement.

Giving medication in the form of pills or powder can best be done as follows: Roll the medication into a little ball of hamburger meat and place it as far back as possible in the beagle's mouth.

Disorders of the Coat and Skin

Beagles shed normally every spring and fall to exchange winter fur for summer fur. Abnormal hair loss does, however, occur as well and can be caused by one of the following: poor feeding, eczema, parasites, a generally poor condition after illness, and hormonal disturbances.

Symptoms can include itch, bare spots, and repeated shedding. Ask your veterinarian for the right treatment. He or she will look into the following:

● The feeding of the beagle can cause a reaction on the skin and coat. Reactions to potatoes, pork, horse meat, herbs, and seasonings are particularly common. Dogs should definitely not be given too much fat.

● Several types of eczema can be caused by excessive carbohydrates in the diet. In any event, leave treatment of eczema to your veterinarian, who will cut the remaining hair from the affected spots, clean the area, and recommend medication against infection. He or she also may recommend an improved diet.

● Another possible cause is parasites, including fleas and lice (see page 26) or worms (see page 50). A much more serious parasite is the scabies mite *(Sarcoptes)*, which buries itself in the skin to lay its eggs. The infested dog scratches itself continuously, resulting in raw bare spots at the elbow, knee, and margins of the ear. If left untreated, the bare spots spread over the whole body.

Parasites must be fought with strong remedies. Generally your veterinarian will recommend a treatment requiring skin baths. To avoid further transmission, separate the affected dog from other animals and maintain proper hygiene (see page 27 for a discussion of ticks and lice).

● Abnormal hair loss often occurs after serious illness. It certainly will help to gradually restore the normal condition of the coat with a proper, accurately balanced diet.

● Baldness (alopecia) in puppies may be caused by a deficiency of thyroxine (thyroxine is an iodine-containing hormone produced by the thyroid gland to regulate metabolism), resulting from an iodine deficiency in the diet of the dam. In any event, consult a veterinarian for advice. Prevent the problem by feeding a pregnant beagle properly.

The mother dog may have problems with baldness after whelping, caused by a hormone deficiency. Again, proper feeding can remedy this quickly.

Disorders of the Digestive System

Constipation

If your beagle doesn't defecate on schedule, there's no reason to be alarmed immediately. You don't need to intervene until the trouble has continued for three days. Then add one of the following laxatives to the feed: Metamulin or Mucilose. These are over-the-counter products—available without prescription. If you feed dry food, add water to it, as well as some mineral oil (1 teaspoon per 10 pounds of body weight). Take care to never give mineral oil for longer than three days.

Diarrhea

Diarrhea is caused mainly by various infectious diseases, poor feeding, poisoning, colds, and intestinal worms. The stools are thin, sometimes slimy, and there may even be blood in serious cases.

Most cases of mild diarrhea can be cured by restricting your pet to weak tea, rice, or rice water for a day. If necessary, medicate the dog with charcoal tablets. Once the diarrhea diminishes, gradually resume normal feeding, provided that this food is proper and is not the cause of the diarrhea.

In a serious case of diarrhea, with slime and blood, you should always consult your veterinarian. In all cases, be sure that the sick beagle lies in a warm place.

Anal Sacs

The anal sacs have small openings that become visible by slightly curling the anus outward. You can notice the two openings at 5 and at 7 o'clock, viewing the anal opening as a watch. The glands continually produce a nasty-smelling fluid that is stored in the sacs until emptied during defecation. The dog can also squeeze the fluid out of the sacs when danger threatens. In othe words, the anal sacs function precisely like the stink glands of the skunk. When the anal sacs do not empty normally, they go from being full to being overfilled (impacted). Next, the fluids become concentrated, leading to a grainy mass containing only a small proportion of liquid. The grains irritate the wall of the anal sacs, and the dog responds by licking under its tail. If that doesn't bring relief, the animal pulls its anus along the ground. We call this symptom "sledding," in which the animal sits, raises its hind legs, and pull itself along with its forelegs.

Sledding can also be caused by other problems, such as feces adhering to the anus, undigested grass that hangs partially out of the intestines, lint-worms, and small wounds. To determine the true cause, examine the beagle under the tail. If the anal sacs are impacted, you can often see a small bump on either side of the anus.

Sledding along the ground scrapes the openings of the sacs, and the resulting damage allows bacteria to enter. These can bring about a nasty infection that will require extensive treatment by your veterinarian.

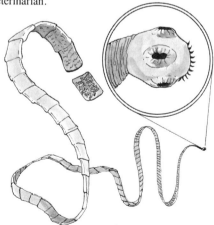

Tapeworm with a close-up of head.

A common side effect of an infection of the anal sacs is a bare back. The affected dog has a terrible itch and scrapes itself wherever it can. Generally the bare spot develops on the rump. This is the same spot that is chafed bare when a dog has fleas. So if you see a bare back, remember to look not only for fleas but also for problems in the anal sacs. If the anal sacs are overfilled, they must be emptied manually—a job best left to your veterinarian. Remember, if this isn't done, there may be all kinds of complications. Anal sac infections can be cured by medication. Some veterinarians also advise an operation to remove the sacs altogether.

Worms

The most common intestinal worms are tapeworms and roundworms.

Tapeworms

Tapeworms attach themselves with the head *(scolex)* to the mucous membranes of the intestines and suck nourishment. The head is connected to a chain of segments *(proglotids,)* and each segment contains a large number of eggs that are excreted with the feces.

Dogs can be infested by at least seven types of tapeworms, one of which, the *Echinococcus* tapeworm, is definitely dangerous to humans. All tapeworms live in the small intestine. Every species of tapeworm has a specific intermediate host for its life cycle. These can be fleas, lice, sheep, pigs, rabbits, hares, or dogs.

The symptoms of tapeworm infestation are obvious only in serious cases. They include weight loss (despite a good diet), excitability, cramps, and sometimes diarrhea. You can detect the segments of tapeworm in the stools as small white pieces. You can also see them as dried pieces resembling rice kernels in the hairs around the anus. Immediately consult a veterinarian. He or she will prescribe remedies against the worm as well as against any fleas present.

If Your Beagle Gets Sick

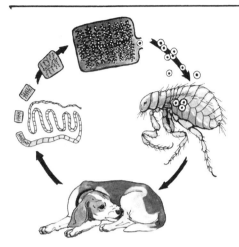

Life cycle of the dog tapeworm. Tapeworm segments containing eggs are passed in the feces.

Roundworms

Roundworms are sturdy and white, ranging in length from 2 to 4 inches (5–10 cm), with the females longer than the males. They also appear in the small intestine.

The eggs are excreted with the stools. When a dog takes in such an egg, it lodges in the intestine. There the egg develops into a larva, which drills itself through the intestinal wall into the bloodstream, by which it is carried to the lungs. It stays there for some time and then travels via the respiratory system to the throat. It is swallowed and then settles in the intestines, where the larva matures to the adult stage.

Damage to the lungs during the process can cause infections. As symptoms, look for digestive disturbances of all types, changing appetite, constipation, diarrhea, intestinal infections, and sometimes also a vomiting of worms. Pups have a hard, swollen stomach; they walk with legs apart, cough, grow thin, and develop a bad, dull coat.

Immediately consult a veterinarian. Prevent infestation by keeping the dog quarters properly clean. Remove feces and disinfect the kennels daily. Examine beagles regularly for worms. Breeding bitches must be wormed 10 days before whelping and 10 days after whelping.

Hookworms

Hookworms are common internal blood-sucking parasites with hooked mouth parts with which they fasten themselves to the intestinal walls of the dog, causing the disease ancylostomiasis. The larvae are activated by the hormonal changes of pregnancy and are carried into the embryos by the bloodstream.

Many infestations occur by way of worm eggs that already infested animals pass in the stool.

The symptoms of hookworm infestation are bloody diarrhea, loss of appetite, vomiting and anemia, and pinkish red gums.

Take the patient to your veterinarian at the first sign of illness (and take a stool sample along in a plastic bag).

Heartworms

Heartworms are transmitted by mosquito bites and live in the right ventricle and pulmonary artery of the heart of dogs and other mammals. Heartworms, which are extremely dangerous internal parasites, can grow up to 14 inches (35.5 cm) in length.

The signs of heartworm disease include fatigue, labored breathing, frequent coughing, and faintness. Unfortunately, these symptoms are often not apparent until the disease has reached a grave stage. Therefore, early diagnosis by a veterinarian is essential.

Coughs and Colds

Cough (Kennel Cough)

Kennel cough is a misleading term, because this virus infection does not occur in kennels only. It is agreed that most infected dogs are indeed found in kennels, but all dogs, including house pets, can get it. Kennel cough is an infection of the throat, the windpipe, and the larynx.

If Your Beagle Gets Sick

Every beagle occasionally barks longer than necessary, so that a throat irritation may result. In kennels, including boarding kennels, dogs incite one another to bark, and homesickness can also cause the dog to bark excessively. When this occurs the mucous membranes of the throat and larynx can become irritated.

Kennel cough, however, is highly contagious. It is caused by a virus, although it can be complicated by a bacterial infection as well. Affected dogs have a basically normal body temperature and remain normally active and alert.

The infection can be prevented by an attenuated vaccine, which normally is administered by the veterinarian in the standard puppy series and the annual booster shot. Dogs with kennel cough should be kept in a quiet place away from other dogs. All causes for barking should be avoided. There are no specific treatments, although cough suppressants are usually recommended.

I strongly suggest that you have the sick dog examined by a veterinarian to be sure it doesn't catch bronchitis. The veterinarian will certainly want to suppress this bacterial infection with antibiotics, because once bacteria invade the body, a lung infection can easily result.

It is always better to have two people take a beagle's temperature. Lift the dog onto a table. Then, one person holds the dog and calms it, while the other lifts up the tail and gently introduces the thermometer into the rectum.

Colds and Chills

There is a great likelihood that your beagle has caught a cold if it stops eating and keeps shivering and its temperature is elevated. It appears everything but happy and looks for a warm spot. Make sure that the dog's sleeping spot isn't exposed to drafts (as when doors or windows are opened) and that it isn't forced to change its position frequently because of heavy traffic in the house. In short, keep the beagle warm and quiet and put it on a light diet. Give it one-quarter of an aspirin tablet crushed in warm milk upon arising and again at night. If the beagle isn't running around normally by the following day, consult your veterinarian. Bear in mind that a dog with chills could be suffering the effects of a serious infectious disease (including distemper or canine hepatitis).

Chills can occur when a beagle is exposed to cold wind for a long period, for example during a hunting expedition. As a result, its temperature drops drastically, perhaps as low as 80° F (27° C). This is called hypothermia.

Serious Diseases

Distemper

Canine distemper is a viral disease that strikes mainly young dogs but also can infect other animals, including raccoons, coyotes, skunks, and wolves. It poses no danger to humans.

The first symptoms of distemper are visible about five to eight days after the virus invades the body. At first, only the mucous membranes are affected. Common symptoms are coughing, sneezing, a drippy nose and teary eyes, and sometimes diarrhea.

Top: Beagles are affectionate little animals, loving humans and practically all kinds of pets alike. Bottom left: This lovely beagle dam was often extremely nervous while nursing her pups. I had to keep her on a leash, meanwhile assuring her that her active and playful puppies were "just doing their thing." Bottom right: after nursing, the pups always ran off to the yard where some extra goodies were awaiting them.

If Your Beagle Gets Sick

The virus then proceeds to invade other tissues and do damage there. At that point, a secondary bacterial infection can significantly worsen the disease picture. The lungs are particularly susceptible, and pneumonia is a real possibility. Bronchitis and pleuritis are also possible, and these symptoms can be so serious as to be fatal.

On rare occasions, skin problems also occur in the form of small bumps on the hairless areas of the stomach. Many authorities dispute whether this is a typical symptom of distemper, however.

The most serious form of the disease appears only after the passage of considerable time. The dog's temperature runs as high as $103°-105°$ F ($39.5°-40.5°$ C); immediate medical attention is required. Without it, distemper enters the nervous system. This brings about a variety of symptoms, ranging from lameness to muscle cramps. In most cases, infections of the nervous system are fatal, and few dogs recover completely. Most survivors are left with a disability, like a limp or an abnormal posture.

Few medicines are effective against distemper. Frequently, antibiotics are prescribed to fight the secondary bacterial infection, but these antibiotics have no effect whatever on the virus. The only medication for distemper is prevention, brought about by a well-planned vaccination schedule.

A well-planned schedule is a complex concept. It is clear that every pup that takes in an adequate amount of mother's milk during the first 24 hours of life is protected against distemper for some time. The puppy acquires immunity and resistance from the mother dog. How long the passive immunity persists depends on the degree of protection that the mother dog herself possesses. If she has little protection, then the puppies become susceptible to distemper within a few weeks of whelping. If she is well protected, the puppies may be protected until the twelfth or thirteenth week of life. Authorities are virtually unanimous in advising that puppies be vaccinated against distemper by the time they are eight weeks old. I recommend the following vaccination schedule.

To maximize maternal protection, vaccinate the female at the start of heat. By the time she is ready to be bred, protection is at its peak, and two months later, the mother dog can provide satisfactory levels of protection in her milk. Under these circumstances, the pups should not need a shot before they are 12 – 13 weeks old, certainly not if you keep them in a reasonably protected environment. If the puppies cannot be restricted to contact with only their mother and their keeper, then vaccinate them at 9 weeks. You should revaccinate at about 13 weeks.

That isn't the end of the story. Your beagle will require annual booster shots to keep the antibody level high. Since 1948, some writers have referred to a special form of distemper as "hard pad" disease. This malady is characterized by an excessive development of horny tissue in the hairless portions of the skin. In serious cases, certain parts become extremely hard, especially the soles of the paws. The thickened, hardened soles appear to cause the affected dog a great deal of pain. It walks very gingerly, as if on hot coals. Even so you can hear the paws thump, especially if the dog is walking on linoleum or other flat, hard floors. Most authorities, however, doubt that hard pad disease is a distinct form of distemper. Whatever the truth, a dog vaccinated against distemper is also protected against hard pad disease.

Hepatitis

Hepatitis is a virus disease that is sometimes fatal. The infected animal loses its appetite, runs a fever, emits a bloody diarrhea, or vomits blood. It is quite obvious that the dog has abdominal pains.

Sometimes the disease has a rapid course: One day the dog looks completely healthy and the next day it is dead. It is clear that a veterinarian needs to be consulted immediately. He or she will administer antibiotics and vitamins and may provide a blood transfusion or infuse other fluids.

Beagle puppies grow rapidly, are easy-going, and clean. They do not form an exclusive relationship with one person but respond to anyone who pays attention to them.

If Your Beagle Gets Sick

Hepatitis can be prevented with an attenuated vaccine, which is commonly provided along with distemper vaccine. A yearly booster is necessary. After the booster shot, the dog is generally sluggish, loses its appetite, and runs an elevated temperature. There is no need to consult a veterinarian.

Leptospirosis

This kidney infection is caused by bacterial organisms (*Leptospira* species). It is infectious to humans and occurs in cattle and rats as well as dogs.

The sick beagle has an obvious temperature, completely loses its appetite, has abdominal pains, vomits, loses weight, frequently shows a weakness of the hind legs, has diarrhea, and wants to drink a lot.

The veterinarian administers antibiotics (penicillin and streptomycin), the necessary fluids, and vitamins. To allow the kidneys the chance to heal properly, the veterinarian may perform peritoneal dialysis.

Proper vaccination with a yearly booster can also prevent this disease and its attendant problems. You may need more frequent boosters (up to six per year) if you live in areas with many infected rats or cattle. The disease spreads by contact with the urine of an infected animal or by drinking or swimming in contaminated water. After vaccination, beagles exhibit the same symptoms as after a hepatitis booster.

Rabies

Rabies or hydrophobia is caused by a potentially fatal virus that is highly concentrated in the saliva of rabid animals, such as foxes, skunks, bats, raccoons, cats and dogs; the virus was first identified by Louis Pasteur in 1881. Rabies is an acute infectious disease of the central nervous system. Many, if not all warm-blooded animals can spread this disease, which is endemic in many countries. Rabies-free countries, such a Britain, Australia, and New Zealand, impose strict quarantine regulations to avoid its spread, and even a current vaccination certificate is required when shipping your beagle across some state lines (ask your veterinarian).

No warm-blooded animal, will get rabies until it is bitten by a rabid animal, or infected by a rabid animal's saliva through an open wound. In man, early symptoms include nausea, fever, malaise, and sore throat. Increased salivation and extreme sensitivity of the skin to temperature changes, of the eyes to light, and ears to sound, are signs very important to early diagnosis.

The incubation period of the rabies virus is usually between 10 and 120 days, but sometimes up to 6 months, depending on the location of the bite and the time it takes the virus to reach the brain.

There are two types of rabies: *dumb rabies* (the dog is far from active, the mouth often hangs open, and there is apt to be a peculiar look in the eyes); and *furious rabies*. In the latter the dog is snappy and irritable, becomes restless, and wanders off to hide in dark places. It often howls and usually attacks and/or bites any human or animal that crosses his path. Seek veterinary attention immediately, and if anyone is bitten by a suspect dog (or other warm-blooded animal), clean the wound with soap or disinfectant at once and consult a physician without delay. Prompt action will save a life! Avoid further injury and inform your local police.

However, there is no treatment for rabies, once symptoms have developed in man or dog! Vaccinations against rabies is strongly advisable for all dogs (see Vaccination Schedule, page 60). This will protect your beloved animal and thus you and your family from this potentially fatal disease.

Pseudorabies

Pseudorabies, also known as Aujeszky's disease, is transmitted to dogs by infected pork, especially the pig's larynx. If pork is mixed with beef, this, too, can be infected. In the past, infected dogs had a serious itch, which currently is observed only in rare cases.

Affected dogs become listless and may vomit and have diarrhea. The illness is hard to diagnose. Unfortunately it is irrevocably fatal for dogs. Dogs that consume an infected larynx often die as quickly as two or three days later. To date, there is no treatment.

If Your Beagle Gets Sick

Prevent infection by keeping dogs out of pig sties; the illness can be transmitted in infected urine. Never feed dogs raw pork and definitely no swine larynx. If you feed pork to dogs that are not allergic to it, boil it in water for at least half an hour.

First Aid

Bites

Beagles are not the biting type, but they do sometimes bite humans or another animal. Males that are kept together in a kennel have been known to inflict painful bites on each other, frequently involving a torn ear. Bite wounds, including those on the ears, can bleed severely.

If your beagle suffers a small wound, wash it with a mild antiseptic. If it needs stitches, or if a wound seems to heal slowly, consult the veterinarian. If there is muscle damage, the wound may take somewhat longer to heal well and certainly will require professional attention.

Note: See your veterinarian immediately if the bite was inflicted by a wild animal or by a dog not immunized against rabies (see page 56).

Insect Stings

Beagles are extremely playful, and they love to chase bees and wasps. No wonder that beagles are subject now and then to a painful sting! Douche the stung area with a strong solution of bicarbonate of soda. Be sure to consult a veterinarian for stings on or near the nose, mouth, or eyes.

Frostbite

Frostbite, which makes the animal shiver and look sleepy, is rare in dogs, even in hunting hounds like beagles. If they have been outside in freezing weather for a long time, however, it is still quite possible that the margins of the ear, the tail, or the scrotum may be touched by frostbite. If you suspect this, put your beagle in a warm room. Place a hot water bottle (in a cover) in its sleeping basket or an electric pad or blanket if available. This helps raise the body temperature. Warm the affected parts with your hands or use a moist,

warm towel (note, that I said *warm*, not *hot!*). Under no circumstances should you rub or squeeze! Give the beagle warm liquids to drink, and check the rectal temperature every hour.

If the animal is unconscious, consult a veterinarian immediately.

Eye Troubles

If your beagle suddenly closes its eyelids, it may have sand or other impurities in the eye. Rinse the eye or eyes carefully with eyewash. If none is available, use milk that has been boiled, cooled, and filtered. Apply with a plastic syringe, which is available in the drugstore. Be sure not to touch the eyeball in the process. When you rinse, be sure you use more than enough rinsing liquid.

If your beagle continues to squeeze its eyelids (or there is no marked improvement), consult your veterinarian because you are probably dealing with an infection of the mucous tissue. Such an infection often results from drafts—for example, if your beagle was permitted to put its head out of the window of a moving vehicle.

Any eye irritation causes heavy tearing, but a heavy flow of tears can also be caused by a blockage in the tear ducts. A veterinarian can flush away the blockage. Stick to the following rule: If excessive tearing persists longer than two hours, consult your veterinarian immediately. A number of eye infections and disorders, such as glaucoma, should be treated only by a veterinarian.

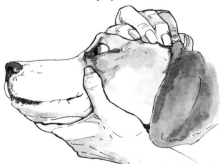

Checking the eye of a beagle. Put your hands around your pet's head and apply gentle pressure to open the eyelid.

If Your Beagle Gets Sick

Taking Your Beagle's Pulse and Heartbeat

As soon as the body temperature of a dog exceeds 103° F (39.5° C), it has a fever. This doesn't always mean that it is sick. The body temperature may rise somewhat because of excitement, or from riding in a hot car, among other reasons. You can take the temperature rectally.

To help establish whether your beagle may require a veterinarian's attention, you can also check the pulse on the front paw on the heartside, or on the upper inside of the thigh. Place your finger lightly on one of these spots for one minute and count the number of beats.

A healthy, grown dog has a pulse rate or heart rate of 70 to 90 beats a minute.

Can Dog Diseases Be Dangerous to Humans?

Yes! Diseases transmissible to humans include leptospirosis and rabies (if a rabid dog inflicts a bite). Therefore, it is always advisable to consult a veterinarian whenever it is unclear from what illness a dog is suffering.

Euthanasia

If your beagle remains healthy and avoids serious accidents, the end of its days will probably occur between its twelfth and fifteenth year.

Unfortunately the saying "Old age has its infirmities" is all too true. An aged beagle tends to become slower in its movements. Its eyesight dims and its teeth fall out. It has trouble holding its urine and its feces, so that it needs to relieve itself more often. Serious illness can become a problem, and you may have to consult a veterinarian. Pain-killing drugs can help and often a carefully regulated diet. Generally, a beagle maintains its interest in food. Even in old age it will greedily attack its rations and swallow them with gusto to the last bite.

The aging process in beagles tends to be gradual, in contrast to the situation with large dogs, which can go from exuberance to infirmity within months. If no serious illness or infirmities occur, you can just quietly await the end of your dog's life.

Vaccination Schedule for Dogs

Disease	Initial Vaccination	Boosters
Adenovirus 2*	8 weeks	12 weeks; annually
Bordetella*	8 weeks	12 weeks; every 6 months
Distemper	8 weeks	12 weeks; 16 weeks; annually
Hepatitis	8 weeks	12 weeks; 16 weeks; annually
Leptospirosis	8 weeks	12 weeks; 16 weeks; annually
Parainfluenza	8 weeks	12 weeks; 16 weeks; annually
Parvovirus	8 weeks	12 weeks; 16 weeks; 6 months or annually, depending upon vaccine used.
Rabies	12 weeks	Every 1-3 years, depending upon local and state ordinances.

* In part responsible for the "kennel cough" syndrome.

58

There are cases, however, in which an animal develops so many ailments that it requires almost constant attention without any clear sign that it will soon die naturally. In such cases, you must seriously consider the possibility of euthanasia. Discuss the situation thoroughly with your veterinarian. Let him or her give you a professional opinion about the remaining possibilities that your beagle's life can be extended for its pleasure and for yours. If no such possibilities remain, then euthanasia may be the best remaining course of action.

At that point, your dog has been your loyal friend and companion for many years, so it is only fair that you stay with it to its last breath and heartbeat. Your dog has the right to spend its last moments in your company.

You need not be afraid of the leave-taking. Death in the office of your veterinarian is a far from scary event. The veterinarian will use personal skills and medications to calm the beagle, so that it falls into a deep sleep. Once asleep, the dog receives a final injection, a strong dose of pain-killing drugs.

At that point, the breathing becomes shallower and the heart beats more slowly. The dog remains asleep until the end.

Once death has occurred, several involuntary reflexes may occur, but they should not upset you. Believe me, at that point your dog is beyond pain and not aware of anything. It has entered into timeless sleep while aware that its master was by its side.

You, yourself will be left with an empty, sad feeling. After all, your faithful companion through the years has disappeared from your life forever. All you have are the memories.

For this reason, I think it best that you acquire another dog. My own experience tells me that it's best to buy a new beagle even before the death of your old one. However, you should be aware that a frisky young pup can make life difficult for your old friend. If that happens, involve yourself intensively with both animals and intervene if the new pup bothers the old dog.

Simple Obedience Training

Obedience training is a continuous process that takes place during the daily interaction between you and your beagle. You and the other members of your family are the only ones who can effectively teach the beagle. Others can help; they can teach you how to teach your dog, but the real work you have to do yourself.

Read several books on the topic, so that you get an idea of the different methods used to teach certain thing to dogs. You will notice that different authors don't always agree and may even contradict one another. In the end, you have to decide which of the applicable methods is best for you. Your two guiding principles should be whether the approach promotes a better relationship between you and your beagle (or, at least, doesn't worsen it!) and whether your dog makes progress as you go along. Remember, theory can be very important, but without practical experience it isn't much use to you. Still, without a theoretical background, you won't be able to interpret many of the developments in the training process properly.

You will obtain considerable practical experience in the daily contact with your beagle, but you should also consider taking your dog to a behavior and obedience training school. It will enlarge your outlook and make you aware of your mistakes. While the instructor teaches you, you will also learn from the mistakes or strengths of other students.

Basic Standards for Pets

As a minimum, your pet should learn to walk alongside you properly while on a leash, to sit, to stay, to lie in a place you select, and to come when you call it. Other desirable "skills" for your beagle depend on your needs.

"Sit"

Many beagles sit down naturally when they want to look up at their master. You can use this tendency by saying "sit" every time the beagle sits

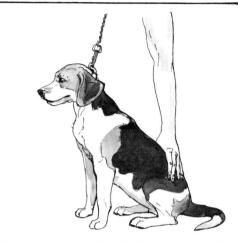

To teach your beagle to "sit," hold its head up by raising the leash, and press down firmly on its rear end.

down on its own. After a while, the dog will make a connection between the word and its action.

This technique makes the beagle basically familiar with the command, but it isn't actually "obedience." A more direct approach is to kneel next to your puppy and hold its collar with your right hand. Then give it the command, "sit," and pull up its head somewhat with your right hand while, with the left, you gradually push down its rump, so that it is forced to sit down. As soon as the dog does this, stroke its head and back quietly and praise it. Say, "That's a good dog, that's 'sit,'" or words to that effect.

If the dog gets the urge to rise, immediately put your left hand back on its rump, push it down, and correct the dog with, "No, sit." Then praise it again as soon as it sits completely.

When you push down the dog, keep your left hand as far back on the rump as possible. Many people make the mistake of putting their hand too far forward, so that, in effect, they push on the loins. This is less effective because you have to push a lot harder, and it is also quite unpleasant for the dog. As a result, it may start to defy you, which naturally is not your intent.

Simple Obedience Training

At the start, don't let your dog sit for too long a time. After it sits properly for a little while, let it go with a pleasantly spoken command, "Free," or whatever word you decide to use to signal release. Then play with your beagle a little while and let it romp around as a reward. Altogether, the "sit" lesson doesn't need to take more than two or three minutes. I strongly recommend keeping all lessons quite short for pups and other dogs starting obedience training. However, during that short time, work intensively. This way, the beagle learns the most, and you avoid the chance that the animal becomes bored. Feel free to repeat the "sit" lesson three or four times per day.

"Stay"

After several days, you won't have to put pressure on the dog's rump anymore; you will be able to stand up while you give the command. As you step away with your right foot, swing your left hand palm down toward your pet's face almost far enough to touch the muzzle, and command, "Stay!" Slowly increase the length of time you

To teach the command "stay," tell your beagle to "sit," then step away with your right foot as you swing your left hand, palm down, toward the dog's muzzle and say, "Stay" in an emphatic tone of voice.

have the beagle stay in place until you give it the command that releases it.

You don't need to set any records. At that stage of training, the most important thing is that your beagle respond immediately to your command and not move until you give the signal by saying, "free"—or whatever.

It is important that your beagle perform the action on command perfectly at least once every day. If your dog obeys some times and other times gets up without permission and runs away, you may have asked more from your beagle than it could handle. Once this occurs you may find that your dog is almost *forced* to make mistakes constantly. Since you have to correct continually, your beagle, rarely if ever receives praise. Very soon it loses all interest in working with you.

It helps to give the first "sit" and "stay" lessons in a quiet room, where there are few distractions. This way, the dog can take in more easily what you are trying to teach. Once the lesson goes smoothly indoors, you can start practicing with your beagle out of doors in a quiet environment. At the same time, you can commence indoors with the "heel" command.

"Heel"

Before you take your beagle out of doors on a leash, it should be used to wearing a collar indoors. In general, this takes a day, or at most several days.

You can get your beagle puppy somewhat used to a leash indoors, also. Connect the leash to the collar and let the puppy drag it behind itself.

When you move out of doors, the puppy will rebel at first against the limiting freedom of the leash. It may make wild jumps, it may lie down or sit down, or it may try to walk backward and pull its head out of the collar. Walk along with your pup and keep the leash from being pulled taut. The puppy should know from the start that the leash is not intended for a "tug of war."

Simple Obedience Training

When "heeling," your beagle walks along on your left, its head about at a level with your left knee. When you practice turns, hold your beagle on a very short leash.

Soon the beagle will be used to the leash. Then you can try to catch its attention with friendly talk. If the puppy starts walking along your left side, then praise it constantly with words like, "That's a good dog. That's 'heel.' Very good!" As long as it keeps walking on your left and the leash stays slack, keep praising the beagle constantly. If it tries to run off and the leash is pulled taut, get the dog to come back to you with one or more *brief* tugs while you give the command, "heel" at short intervals. As soon as the beagle once again walks along with you properly, praise it lavishly.

Naturally, you can't expect perfection from your puppy. The most important result of this lesson is that your puppy begins to understand clearly that it will constantly be rewarded if it walks along beside you.

Don't let this lesson go on too long, either. A few minutes at a time is really enough. Very gradually, you can make the exercise somewhat more difficult. Then, for example, you can teach your beagle to sit down close to you as soon as you stand still. To make left and right turns, hold the

dog on a very short leash. This forces your pet to turn with you. Command "heel" as you make the turn.

If you experience any difficulty teaching your dog to "heel" properly, you should go to an obedience-training course. The practical help that a good instructor can give can't be replaced even by a good book.

"Lie Down"

"Lie down" or more simply "Down," can be a lifesaving command for your beagle. Sooner or later your dog will be off leash when a car is approaching. If you call the dog to come, you might call it in front of the wheels of the oncoming car. It is far safer if you can get the beagle to stay where it is with the command, "lie down," appropriately followed by the command, "stay."

Lying down for someone of higher rank is a gesture of submission. If you force your beagle to lie down, this represents a gesture of domination, and your beagle may find the reason for it hard to understand. There's a good chance, therefore, that your dog will not react dependably while it is still learning the concept of "lie down." Therefore, don't impose this demand too forcefully, for it will inevitably make your dog more unsure.

Make good use of situations when your puppy lies down beside you on its own, perhaps to be stroked. Kneel down by the dog, and with a rather deep voice, say "Lie down" while you quietly stroke it. Follow by saying, "Good dog. That's 'Lie down.' Stay. Good dog." If the beagle then wants to get up, you can push it down again and repeat the command "lie down," again followed by quiet conversation and strokes.

Don't let your puppy lift the command on its own. Keep it in position until you tell your dog,

Top: The beagle belongs to the group of scent hounds— dogs that hunt primarily by using their sense of smell. Bottom: When two dogs that are not acquainted meet, the very first thing they do is touch noses. This preliminary testing determines "on the spot" whether the dogs are going to like each other.

Simple Obedience Training

"free," and then romp a little with it. Once again, however, don't let the training session last too long.

The next step is to kneel down by a dog that's standing, give the command, "sit," and take hold of a front leg with each of your hands and, by pulling gently, force the dog to lie while you give the command, "lie down."

As your puppy starts to understand better and better what the commands, "lie down" and "stay" mean, gradually stop stroking the dog the whole time. Don't remain in a kneeling position, but get on your feet. You can still stand bent over your beagle, with a hand stretched down toward the dog. This is also a dominating gesture, but your dog should be getting accustomed to this situation and adapt to it. Still, your posture, bent over the dog, will impress the beagle enough to keep it in its place.

Now the concept of "lie down" will be understood in principle, but you need to refine it by applying it in gradually more difficult situations. The command will come to mean that the beagle is to lie down immediately and to stay down, regardless whether there are other people or other dogs around. Again, the best way to learn this is in a group under the leadership of a good instructor.

"Come"

If you want your beagle to come as soon as you call it, you must take care to avoid a few mistakes at all costs.

1. Never call your dog to come when you think it likely that it won't do so. If your dog is just learning this concept, it will unlearn it because it gets the idea that your calling can safely be ignored.

2. Never chase your beagle to catch it if it doesn't respond to your call. Most dogs love to

The beagle is not only gentle and lovable but very responsive, naturally curious, alert, intelligent, and of an even temperament. This attentive dog, who was just told to "sit," is eagerly awaiting the next command.

play tag, and your beagle will take your attempts to catch it as an invitation to a game and do its best to keep out of reach. So, do the opposite. Move away from your beagle. Perhaps even squat and hide behind a bush while the dog looks on. This will stimulate the puppy to come to you.

3. No matter how angry you may get, don't try to correct your dog by yelling at it when it comes up to you. This only scares the dog away. No matter how hard this is for you, control yourself and praise your dog when it comes to you after you called it. Also, never call the dog to you when you intend to punish it.

Your beagle needs to understand that something pleasant will occur if it comes to you after having been called. The pleasant consequence doesn't always have to be a treat. In fact, I think it better not to reward constantly by feeding treats. You can just as well give a hug, or play with the dog, or simply talk to it in a high, soft voice, giving it praise and strokes.

Make use of those situations when you can safely predict that your dog is going to come toward you. For example, at feeding time, call the dog in a high and friendly tone while you are holding the feeding dish so that the dog can see what you are doing. If it comes, speak to it with praise, stroke it, and then give it the dish with food. Similarly, as you get ready to go out with your dog, you will have little difficulty getting your beagle to come to you. So, make use of all common situations when you know your beagle will want to come toward you in order to teach the concept of "come." Each time, try everything you can think of to make it worthwhile for your beagle to come to you. This sets up the best conditions for a speedy, pleasant lesson in coming when called.

"Let Go"

A beagle pup should learn to accept early that at the command "let go" it should allow you to take away whatever it is playing with. At first the puppy will growl and try to defend its "booty."

Simple Obedience Training

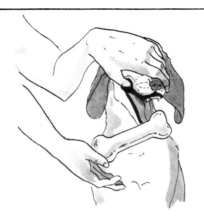

"Let go." You must convince the beagle pup while it is still young that you are the stronger of the two and that it must give up anything you ask for without protest.

This is just the way it behaved with its siblings, against which it had to assert itself to avoid being shoved into the background. In other words, it is a natural reaction, but you should not let it go unchecked. If you do, you will be sorry when it picks up some splintery bone that you must get away from it so it will not be hurt. You must convince the puppy while it is still young that you are the stronger and that it must give up without protest anything you ask for. Practice this first with a toy your puppy is particularly fond of. Get your dog to play with the toy, and then take it away with a curt "let go." Praise its cooperation immediately. Practice with other objects, eventually even with its full dish of food.

Your dog will learn to accept this "game" or will at least not find it unusual to give up whatever it has between its teeth when told to do so. Never use force when practicing this exercise.

Understanding Beagles

The beagle belongs to the *hound* breeds, which can be split into two groups (1) The scent hounds or scent followers and (2) the sight hounds or sight hunters.

The beagle is by far the best known representative of the scent followers and one of the oldest representatives of the scent-following tracking dogs. The breed probably dates back to pre-Roman times.

In the United States, we recognize two sizes of beagles: 13 inches or under, and over 13 but under 15 inches. The weight limit for dogs under 13 inches is 18 pounds; for dogs over 13 inches, it is 20 pounds.

Dog experts often say, correctly, that the beagle is a carbon copy of the harrier and the English foxhound. Both these breeds are considerably larger than the beagle, especially the English foxhound. This makes it all the more important not to breed oversized beagles, meaning individuals that are more than 15 inches. It makes no sense at all to try to turn a beagle into a foxhound!

Although a beagle may have any color, most members of the breed are black, white, or tan, with different combinations and markings. The coat is close and of medium length and will remain glossy with good daily care. The tail of a healthy beagle is carried gaily, but not curled squirrel style; the ears are set at eye level, drop beside the cheeks, and have "fine leather." The skull is domed and moderately wide, with an indication of peak. The medium-length muzzle should not be snippy. To maintain the true appearance and character traits of the beagle it is extremely important to breed with the utmost care.

Beagles are quite popular. Some 50,000 new individuals are registered annually with the American Kennel Club, and this figure is only the tip of the iceberg. Each year, many tens of thousands of additional beagles are born. So there is real danger that breed quality may suffer.

If you want to acquire a beagle (see page 7), don't even consider the mass-produced puppies. If you personally know a dependable pet store or breeder, fine. If not, start by contacting the AKC for assistance (see address on page 76). They will give you the address of the headquarters of the local beagle club. They, in turn, will be more than willing to give you a list of reputable, AKC-approved breeders in your area.

Remember that the beagle has remained popular through the years, despite the competition, because of its many excellent qualities and valued traits. Two of its very outstanding qualities are certainly endurance and courage. It is difficult, perhaps impossible, to find a breed that excels the beagle on these points. The beagle in the field is almost as well known in America as in Europe, although we know the breed somewhat better as a house pet.

As a house pet, the beagle still distinguishes itself by several excellent qualities. As I said earlier, beagles and children are almost inseparable, and the charming and intelligent beagles are also generally affectionate toward other pets (see page 20). They are always ready to be on the go, and from excitement and pure joy they often sound their lovely hound voice.

You will have to set limits on this enthusiastic vocalization if you keep a beagle in the city as you don't want trouble with the neighbors. If you

The beagle is a natural hunter.

acquire the dog when it is young, you can train it fairly easily even though a beagle, as a natural hunter, derives an unimaginable deal of pleasure from a loud howling session now and then. This is particularly true if it is left alone, but if you start when the dog is young, you shouldn't run into any serious problems.

The beagle is definitely a suitable city hound. It certainly loves to be outside often and will thankfully accept any opportunity to be taken for a walk or to romp out-of-doors. As you walk through the streets, you can depend on the beagle's natural calm as well as its proverbial loyalty. Believe me, the beagle doesn't care at all about bad weather or rough terrain; you can take your dog wherever you want, secure in the knowledge that nothing will wear it down.

If you are a hunter, the beagle is hard to beat. Almost any type of upland game arouses its interest, including cottontail rabbit, squirrel, and pheasant, which are its favorite. If you train the beagle properly, you can derive an enormous amount of pleasure from your helper. Professional trainers often can be of indispensable assistance in developing your beagle as a hunter (see page 69).

History

Legend has it that beagles, those "merry little hounds with big hearts," descended from hounds used by King Arthur and his knights. Some say their ancestors came to England with William the Conqueror.

It isn't easy, however, to establish exactly when the breed first made its appearance. It is known that the ancient Greeks used so-called scenting hounds for the hunt 400 years or so before Christ. The dogs, which were of several different breeds, hunted in packs with their keepers. In England and Wales this type of hunt was also known about 1400 A.D. The pack consisted not only of scent followers but also included sight hounds, such as grayhounds. In fact, it wasn't until 1550 that people started differentiating among the various types of scent hounds. For example, people trained the

Legend has it that beagles, from the French *biegles,* meaning small, descended from hounds brought to England by the knights of William the Conqueror—as shown in this fragment from an ancient tapestry.

large hounds, the so-called buck hounds, to hunt deer and other large game. The small hounds were used to hunt hares, rabbits, and pheasants; and these small dogs were called beighs or beagles, from the French beigle, meaning *small*. This doesn't mean, however, that the dogs that were called beagles 400 years ago were the same dogs we call beagles today. Representations of beagles from the sixteenth, seventeenth and eighteenth centuries show that clearly. The dogs varied in height between 5 and 25 inches (13–63.5 cm).

In this connection, it's interesting to note that in the days of King Henry VIII (1491–1547) and even more so during the reign of his daughter, Elizabeth I (1558–1603), the then miniature beagles were transported to the hunting fields in the panniers of saddles or in the pockets of hunting coats.

One supposes that the beagle resulted from experiments in crossing the harrier with the Southern hound. It's no surprise that in the "early

Understanding Beagles

days" beagles were often called "little harriers." Over time, breeders selected the larger individuals from among these dogs, creating a breed that was 19–21 inches (48–53.5 cm) in height. Continuous selection, using, in turn, only the smallest individuals for breeding, gradually resulted in a dog of reduced size, a miniature breed called Queen Bess. These dogs proved to be too small for hunting, and they rapidly lost popularity. Breeders continued their experiments, and gradually the first "true" beagle developed in two types the shallow-flewed and the deep-flewed, depending on the depth of the upper lip. The first type is supposed to have been the faster, and the second, the one with the more musical voice and the more assured manner.

The present-day beagle received a number of characteristics from several other breeds. Its keen nose is supposedly derived from the Kerry beagle, a miniature bloodhound, and all its other traits were acquired by crossing foxhounds and coonhounds.

It wasn't until about 1860 that the first well-proportioned beagles were introduced to the United States. One of the known participants was General Richard Rowett of Carlinville, Illinois, who brought several good representatives of the breed from England, including the now famous Rosey and Dolly.

Beagles were known in North America before then, but they were far from ideal individuals, especially in size. The dogs brought over by Rowett and others were used in a professional selective breeding program that resulted in superior beagles within several years. They were able to meet all competitors, including those from England.

It wasn't until 1887, however, that the American/English Beagle Club was formed. The standard of the breed was drafted by General Rowett, Norman Elmore of Granby, Connecticut—famous for his marvelous beagle Ringwood, which also came from England—and Dr. L. H. Twadell of Philadelphia, Pennsylvania. These gentlemen acquitted themselves so well of their task that their standard with several minor changes, continues to be used today by the National Beagle Club of America. Even the standard used in England differs only slightly from the one devised by the three U.S. pioneers.

Shortly after the turn of the century, the interest in beagles increased to an amazing extent, and many enthusiastic beagle lovers had privately owned packs. Well-known are the Hempstead, Round Hill, Thornfield, Rockridge, Dungannon, Somerset, Wolver, Piedmont, Old Westbury, and Windholme beagles.

The first beagle field trials were held November 4, 1890, at Hyannis, Massachusetts, and November 7, 1890, at Salem, New Hampshire. Mr. Frank Forest was the winner of the all-age stake for dogs 15 inches and under, and a dog called Tone, owned by the Glenrose Kennels, won the stake for bitches 15 inches and under. Belle Rose, owned by B.S. Turpin, was the winner of the stake for bitches 13 inches and under.

The next year, the number of entries was considerably larger, and from then on one can say that nothing could stop the popularity of the beagle.

Beagles For Work in the Field

Several beagle lovers have made a profession of training beagles for work in the field. Many of these trainers now take their charges over a regular circuit of field trials. They generally start in early fall and continue into late spring.

Field trial clubs plan their events so as not to conflict with one another. This makes it possible to take part in different events each year. Generally, they allow enough time between dates to give dogs a well-earned rest and to allow them a tune-up before the next event.

Your beagle club can tell you where you can find professional trainers. Remember that generally they have more than enough business, so that you will need several names.

At bench shows and field trials, beagles are subdivided into two classes: dogs 15 inches in height or under and those 13 inches or under. After reading our standards discussion (see page 75), it

Understanding Beagles

will be clear that beagles over 15 inches are automatically disqualified from competition.

It certainly would be well worth your time to visit a beagle trial sometime, even if you don't like to hunt. During field trials, beagles are run in braces (meaning pairs). The names of individual hounds are placed on single slips of paper and drawn from a receptacle, the first beagle drawn running with the second hound drawn, and so on. After all braces have been run, the judges may call back any competing beagle that they wish to see again and brace them in any manner they desire; often they make an animal run a second, third, or even fourth time. I have been at competitions where they made certain dogs run eight times. In the end, all judges will have determined the best performers on that particular occasion.

Most generally, the cottontail rabbit is used as game, although it can happen that hares are used.

You can easily imagine that not all beagles are equally adept at hunting; some may be easily distracted for one reason or another, or become nervous and perform poorly. If a beagle has to compete in a strange country it may be put off its stroke. It can also happen that one beagle runs away with all the prizes at the field trial.

A young beagle with true determination is just about the ideal hound. Its natural desire to hunt constitutes the germ for success, with the proper training. The trainer tries to get the beagle to follow a comparatively cold trail until the quarry has gone to earth or has been caught. The young beagle must be the type to enjoy working in rough, unknown territory, irrespective of the weather.

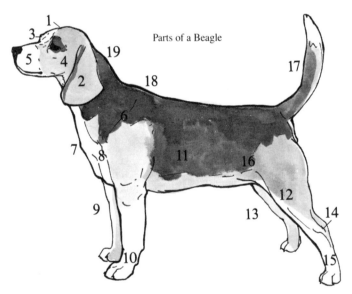

Parts of a Beagle

1. Skull	8. Brisket	15. Rear pastern
2. Ears	9. Forequarters	16. Loin
3. Stop	10. Front pastern	17. Tail
4. Cheek	11. Ribcage	18. Withers
5. Muzzle	12. Stifle	19. Neckline
6. Shoulder	13. Hindquarters	
7. Chest	14. Hock	

Understanding Beagles

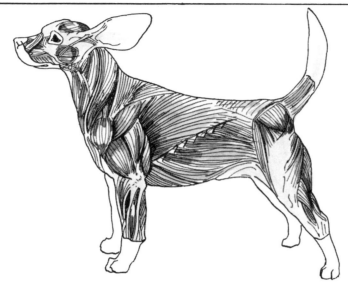

Musculature of the beagle. Though it is a fairly small dog, the beagle is powerfully built.

It is safe to say that a good beagle thrives on work, and the more it goes hunting with its master and its pack, the more it enjoys the chase. Even if you don't hunt, I think it will still be an unforgettable experience to see a pack of beagles hunt. They truly deserve the name I heard somewhere, "music makers of the meadows."

Beagle Shows

Every year there are local and regional shows for beagle hounds. Using the breed standard as a basis, the judges evaluate and grade beagles on their general appearance, physique, bearing, and behavior. Apart from evaluation of the animals, beagle shows (or dog shows, in general) offer a wealth of information. Manufacturers of dog foods offer samples of the latest brands, usually at no or little cost. Useful accessories for beagle owners are also on display. Contacts with other beagle owners are quickly formed, and a lively exchange of experience and information is soon underway. The judges give tips and suggestions for the care and management of your beagle.

If you would like to enter your beagle in a show, check your club publications for dates and send in your application (available from the American Beagle Club; see page 76) and entry fee in good time. Before the judging, you will have to supply the judges with your beagle's pedigree, certificate of health (the local public health authorities often require this, too), and certificate of immunization. For further details, inquire at your local beagle club. Do not go to the show expecting your dog to garner a prize or even come off with a particularly good evalation. The judges are very strict and are chary with prizes.

Description and Standard (adopted by the American Beagle Club and approved by the AKC)

Head: The skull should be fairly long, slightly domed at occiput, with cranium broad and full.

Understanding Beagles

Ears: Ears set on moderately low, long, reaching when drawn out nearly, if not quite, to the end of the nose; fine in texture, fairly broad—with almost complete absence of erectile power—setting close to the head, with the forward edge slightly inturning to the cheek—rounded at tip.

Eyes: Eyes large, set well apart; soft and houndlike; expression gentle and pleading; of a brown or hazel color.

Muzzle: Muzzle of medium length, straight and square-cut; the stop moderately defined.

Jaws: Level. Lips free from flews; nostrils large and open.

Defects: A very flat skull, narrow across the top; excess of dome; eyes small, sharp, and terrierlike or prominent and protruding; muzzle long, snippy or cut away decidedly below the eyes, or very short. Roman-nosed, or upturned, giving a

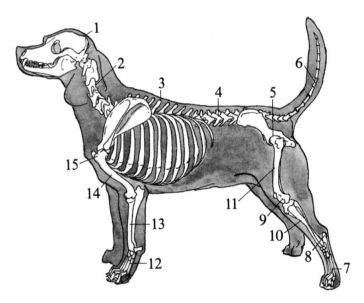

This drawing of a beagle's skeleton shows the most important bones and joints.

1. Occiput
2. Cervical vertebrae
3. Withers
4. Vertebrae column
5. Hip joint
6. Tail vertebrae
7. Back foot or metatarsus
8. Tarsus or hock
9. Stifle or knee
10. Lower thigh (tibia and fibula)
11. Upper thigh (femur)
12. Pastern or metacarpus
13. Forearm (radius and ulna)
14. Upper-arm (humerus)
15. Shoulder joint

Understanding Beagles

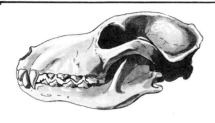

The skull of a beagle should be fairly long and slightly domed at occiput.

dish-faced expression. Ears short, set on high or with a tendency to rise above the point of origin.

Body, Neck and Throat: Neck rising free and light from the shoulders, strong in substance yet not loaded, of medium length. The throat clean and free from folds of skin; a slight wrinkle below the angle of the jaw, however, may be allowable.

Defects: A thick, short neck carried on a line with the top of the shoulders. Throat showing dewlap and folds of skin to a degree termed "throatiness."

Scale of Points

	Points	*Total*
Head		
Skull	5	
Ears	10	
Eyes	5	
Muzzle	5	25
Body		
Neck	5	
Chest and shoulders	15	
Back, loin, and ribs	15	35
Running Gear		
Forelegs	10	
Hips, thighs, and hind legs	10	
Feet	10	30
Coat	5	
Stern	5	10
		100

Varieties

There shall be two varieties: the 13 inch which shall be for hounds not exceeding 13 inches in height and the 15 inch, which shall be for hounds over 13 but not exceeding 15 inches in height.

Disqualification

Any hound measuring more than 15 inches shall be disqualified.

Understanding Beagles

The body of the beagle should be compact, not too short and not too long, but in proportion. The illustrations (from top to bottom) show a sway, a roach, and a long back. It is permissible for a female to have a longer back than a male.

Shoulders and Chest: Shoulders sloping, clean, muscular, not heavy or loaded—conveying the idea of freedom of action with activity and strength. Chest deep and broad, but not broad enough to interfere with the free play of the shoulders.

Defects: Straight, upright shoulders. Chest disproportionately wide or with lack of depth.

Back, Loin, and Ribs: Back short, muscular, and strong. Loin broad and slightly arched, and the ribs well sprung, giving abundance of lung room.

Defects: Very long, swayed, or roached back. Flat, narrow loin. Flat ribs.

Forelegs: Straight, with plenty of bone in proportion to size of the hound. Pasterns short and straight.

Feet: Close, round, and firm. Pad full and hard.

Defects: Out at elbows. Knees knuckled over forward or bent backward. Forelegs crooked or dachshundlike. Feet long, open or spreading.

Hips, Thighs, Hind Legs, and Feet: Hips and thighs strong and well muscled, giving abundance of propelling power. Stifles strong and well let down. Hocks firm, symmetrical, and moderately bent. Feet close and firm.

Defects: Cowhocks or straight hocks. Lack of muscle and propelling power. Open feet.

Tail: Set moderately high; carried gaily, but not turned forward over the back; with slight curve; short compared with size of the hound's tail; with brush.

Defects: A long tail. Teapot curve or inclined forward from the root. Rat tail with absence of brush.

Coat: A close, hard, hound coat of medium length.

Defects: A short, thin coat, or of a soft quality.

Color: Any true hound color.

General Appearance: A miniature foxhound, solid and big for its inches, with the wear-and-tear look of the hound that can last in the chase and follow its quarry to the death.

A beagle pack, eager for the chase.

74

Understanding Beagles

Pack of Beagles (American Standard)

Scale of Points

Hounds: General levelness of pack	40
Hounds: Individual merit of hounds	30
	70
Hounds: Manners	20
Appointments	10
Total	100

Levelness of Pack
The first thing to be considered in a pack is that they present a unified appearance. The hounds must be as near to the same height, weight, conformation, and color as possible.

Individual Merit of the Hounds
This is the individual bench show quality of the hounds. A very level and sporty pack can be brought together and not a single hound be a good beagle. This is to be avoided.

Manners
The hounds must all work gaily and cheerfully, with flags up, obeying all commands cheerfully. They should be broken to heel up, kennel up, follow promptly, and stand. Cringing, sulking, and lying down are to be avoided. Also, a pack must not work as though in terror of the master and whips. In beagle packs it is recommended that the whip be used as little as possible.

Appointments
Master and whips should be dressed alike, the master or huntsman to carry the horn; the whips and master to carry light thong whips. One whip should carry extra couplings on a shoulder strap.

Recommendations for Show Livery
Black velvet cap, white stock, green coat, white breeches or knickerbockers, green or black stockings, white spats, black or dark brown shoes. Vest and gloves optional. Women wear a white skirt instead of white breeches but otherwise should turn out in exactly the same manner.

Useful Addresses

American Beagle Club*
P.O. Box 121
Essex, VT 05451

National Beagle Club*
Mr. John W. Oelsner, Secretary
8 Baldwin Place
Westport, CT 06880

American Kennel Club
51 Madison Avenue
New York, NY 10038

Australian National Kennel Club
Royal Show Grounds
Ascot Vale
Victoria
Australia

Canadian Kennel Club
111 Eglington Avenue
Toronto 12, Ontario
Canada

Irish Kennel Club
41 Harcourt Street
Dublin 2
Ireland

The Kennel Club
1-4 Clargis Street
Picadilly
London, W7Y 8AB
England

New Zealand Kennel Club
P.O. Box 523
Wellington
New Zealand

*These addresses may change as new officers are elected. The latest listing can always be obtained from the American Kennel Club.

Index

Index

Perfect for Pet Owners!

PET OWNER'S MANUALS

Over 50 illustrations per book
(20 or more color photos),
72-80 pp., paperback.

AFRICAN GRAY PARROTS (3773-1)
AMAZON PARROTS (4035-X)
BANTAMS (3687-5)
BEAGLES (3829-0)
BEEKEEPING (4089-9)
BOXERS (4036-8)
CANARIES (2614-4)
CATS (2421-4)
CHINCHILLAS (4037-6)
CHOW-CHOWS (3952-1)
COCKATIELS (2889-9)
COCKATOOS (4159-3)
DACHSHUNDS (2888-0)
DOBERMAN PINSCHERS (2999-2)
DWARF RABBITS (3669-7)
FEEDING AND SHELTERING
    BACKYARD BIRDS (4252-2)
FEEDING AND SHELTERING
    EUROPEAN BIRDS (2858-9)
FERRETS (2976-3)
GERBILS (3725-1)
GERMAN SHEPHERDS (2982-8)
GOLDEN RETRIEVERS (3793-6)
GOLDFISH (2975-5)
GUINEA PIGS (2629-2)
HAMSTERS (2422-2)
LABRADOR RETRIEVERS (3792-8)
LHASA APSOS (3950-5)
LIZARDS IN THE TERRARIUM
    (3925-4)
LONG-HAIRED CATS (2803-1)
LOVEBIRDS (3726-X)
MICE (2921-6)
MUTTS (4126-7)
MYNAS (3688-3)
PARAKEETS (2423-0)
PARROTS (2630-6)
PERSIAN CATS (4405-3)
PIGEONS (4044-9)
PONIES (2856-2)
POODLES (2812-0)
RABBITS (2615-2)

SCHNAUZERS (3949-1)
SHEEP (4091-0)
SHETLAND SHEEPDOGS (4264-6)
SIBERIAN HUSKIES (4265-4)
SNAKES (2813-9)
SPANIELS (2424-9)
TROPICAL FISH (2686-1)
TURTLES (2631-4)
YORKSHIRE TERRIERS (4406-1)
ZEBRA FINCHES (3497-X)

NEW PET HANDBOOKS

Detailed, illustrated profiles (40-60
color photos), 144 pp., paperback.

NEW AQUARIUM HANDBOOK
    (3682-4)
NEW BIRD HANDBOOK (4157-7)
NEW CAT HANDBOOK (2922-4)
NEW COCKATIEL HANDBOOK
    (4201-8)
NEW DOG HANDBOOK (2857-0)
NEW DUCK HANDBOOK (4088-0)
NEW FINCH HANDBOOK (2859-7)
NEW GOAT HANDBOOK (4090-2)
NEW PARAKEET HANDBOOK
    (2985-2)
NEW PARROT HANDBOOK (3729-4)
NEW RABBIT HANDBOOK (4202-6)
NEW SOFTBILL HANDBOOK
    (4075-9)
NEW TERRIER HANDBOOK
    (3951-3)

CAT FANCIER'S SERIES

Authoritative, colorful guides (over
35 color photos), 72 pp., paperback.

BURMESE CATS (2925-9)
LONGHAIR CATS (2923-2)

FIRST AID FOR PETS

Fully illustrated, colorful guide, 20 pp.,
Hardboard with hanging chain and
    index tabs.

FIRST AID FOR YOUR CAT (5827-5)
FIRST AID FOR YOUR DOG (5828-3)

REFERENCE BOOKS

Comprehensive, lavishly illustrated
references (60-300 color photos),
136-176 pp., hardcover & paperback

AQUARIUM FISH SURVIVAL
    MANUAL (5686-8), hardcover
AUSTRALIAN FINCHES, THE
    COMPLETE BOOK OF (6091-1),
    hardcover
BEST PET NAME BOOK EVER, THE
    (4258-1), paperback
CAT CARE MANUAL (5765-1),
    hardcover
COMMUNICATING WITH YOUR
    DOG (4203-4), paperback
COMPLETE BOOK OF
    BUDGERIGARS (6059-8),
    hardcover
COMPLETE BOOK OF PARROTS
    (5971-9), hardcover
DOG CARE, THE COMPLETE BOOK
    OF (4158-5), paperback
DOG CARE MANUAL (5764-3),
    hardcover
GOLDFISH AND ORNAMENTAL
    CARP (5634-5), hardcover
HORSE CARE MANUAL (5795-3),
    hardcover
LABYRINTH FISH (5635-3),
    hardcover
NONVENOMOUS SNAKES (5632-9),
    hardcover
WATER PLANTS IN THE AQUARIUM
    (3926-2), paperback

GENERAL GUIDE BOOKS

Heavily illustrated with color photos,
144 pp., paperback.

COMMUNICATING WITH YOUR DOG
    (4203-4)
DOGS (4158-5)

ISBN prefix: 0-8120

Order from your favorite book or pet store

Barron's Educational Series, Inc. • P.O. Box 8040, 250 Wireless Blvd., Hauppauge, NY 11788
Call toll-free: 1-800-645-3476, in NY: 1-800-257-5729 • In Canada: Georgetown Book Warehouse
34 Armstrong Ave., Georgetown, Ont. L7G 4R9 • Call toll-free: 1-800-668-4336

Be Ready To Save Your Pet's Life

With These Expert Manuals From Barron's...

First Aid For Your Dog

By *Fredric L. Frye, D.V.M., M.S.*
In this clearly-written guide with instructive illustrations, color-coded index tabs quickly point you to vital first aid techniques such as how to: give a heart massage and artificial respiration • stop bleeding • treat frostbite, convulsions and much more. (5828-3)

First Aid For Your Cat

By *Fredric L. Frye, D.V.M., M.S.*
This fully-illustrated, clear guide uses color-coded index tabs to give you quick access to life-saving steps such as how to: restrain and lift an injured cat • give artificial respiration • apply splints and tourniquets • treat gagging, poisoning and much more. (5827-5)

Each Book: Hardboard with hanging chain and index tabs, 20 pp., $9.95, Can. $13.95